Literature in Perspective

General Editor: Kenneth Grose

W. H. Auden

Literature in Perspective

W. H. Auden

Dennis Davison

Evans Brothers Limited, London

Published by Evans Brothers Limited

Montague House, Russell Square, London, W.C.1

© Dennis Davison 1970

First published 1970

Set in 11 on 12 point Bembo and printed in Great Britain by The Camelot Press Ltd., London and Southampton

0 237 35150 1 cased

237 35151 x limp

PR 2455

Literature in Perspective

Reading is a pleasure; reading great literature is a great pleasure, which can be enhanced by increased understanding, both of the actual words on the page and of the background to those words, supplied by a study of the author's life and circumstances. Criticism should try to foster understanding in both aspects.

Unfortunately for the intelligent layman and young reader alike, recent years have seen critics of literature (particularly academic ones) exploring slender ramifications of meaning, exposing successive levels of association and reference, and multiplying the types of ambiguity unto seventy times seven.

But a poet is 'a man speaking to men', and the critic should direct his efforts to explaining not only what the poet says, but also what sort of man the poet is. It is our belief that it is impossible to do the first without doing the second.

Literature in Perspective, therefore, aims at giving a straightforward account of literature and of writers—straightforward both in content and in language. Critical jargon is as far as possible avoided; any terms that must be used are explained simply; and the constant preoccupation of the authors of the Series is to be lucid.

It is our hope that each book will be easily understood, that it will adequately describe its subject without pretentiousness so that the intelligent reader who wants to know about Donne or Keats or Shakespeare will find enough in it to bring him up to date on critical estimates.

Even those who are well read, we believe, can benefit from a lucid expression of what they may have taken for granted, and perhaps—dare it be said?—not fully understood.

K. H. G.

W. H. Auden

Some poets are too elusive for the critic's pedantic net. As you cautiously unstopper the chloroform bottle and prepare to render them insensible, before fixing them for ever behind glass in your private museum, there is a flutter of wings and somehow they have once more escaped. I am rather glad that Auden has always evaded captivity—either by his admirers or by his detractors.

Although I have tried to present the amazing range of Auden's talent—Freudian protest verse, left-wing moralising, horrific ballads, cabaret songs, short love lyrics, long philosophical satires, serious blues and comic religious meditations—in order to assess his poetic status, I have constantly found myself liking one poem immensely, only to turn the page and be equally irritated with another. Is Auden simply an uneven writer, or is he just too versatile for any one reader to appreciate? At all events one can be sure that two pages later there will be something entirely different again. I think it is this unpredictability about each new Auden poem which makes him distinctive. Mere novelty of technique or topic could, of course, prove a superficial attraction: Auden's perpetual variety is refreshing because it springs from a genuine quest for wisdom allied to an insatiable delight in words.

I would like to thank W. H. Auden for his kind replies to my queries: Geoffrey Grigson and Rex Warner for generously supplying personal comments on Auden: my colleague, Alec King, who was at Oxford with Day-Lewis and Auden, and who has loaned me books and helped me in several ways: and many friends who have aided my research or the preparation of the typescript—Margaret Plant, Sadie Stephens, Betty Moore, Marion Adams, Helen Thomson, Ian Laurenson, Carl Stead,

Maureen Mann. I am very grateful to Kenneth Grose for his stimulating editorial advice.

Quotations are taken from the first edition in which the work appeared, unless otherwise stated. Readers using later editions may find slight differences in line numbers, due to deletions or additions, in one or two poems.

D. D.

Acknowledgements

The author and publishers would like to thank the author and Faber and Faber Limited for their permission to quote from the works of W. H. Auden. American rights are as follows: quotations from the works of W. H. Auden are protected by copyright and have been reprinted here by permission of the publisher, Random House, Inc. From *The Dog Beneath the Skin* by W. H. Auden and Christopher Isherwood. Copyright 1935 and renewed 1963 by W. H. Auden and Christopher Isherwood. Reprinted by permission of Random House, Inc. From *The Ascent of F6* by W. H. Auden and Christopher Isherwood. Copyright 1936, 1937 and renewed 1964 by W. H. Auden and Christopher Isherwood. Reprinted by permission of Random House Inc. From *On the Frontier*, by W. H. Auden and Christopher Isherwood. Reprinted by permission of Random House, Inc.

They would also like to thank the authors and Faber and Faber Limited for permission to quote from the works of George Barker, Louis MacNeice, Charles Madge and Stephen Spender. The quotations from *The Magnetic Mountain* by C. Day-Lewis are reprinted by permission of the author, Jonathan Cape Limited and The Hogarth Press. The quotation from *On the Twentieth Anniversary of Soviet Power* by C. Day-Lewis is reprinted by permission of A. D. Peters & Co. The quotation from *World Within World* copyright © by Stephen Spender, Hamish Hamilton, London 1951, is reprinted by permission of the publishers.

They are grateful to Central Press Photos Limited for the cover photograph, to *Plays and Players* and Pollard and Crowther for the photograph from *The Dog Beneath the Skin*, and to the Radio Times Hulton Picture Library for the photographs of Auden, Day-Lewis and Spender, and of Auden and Isherwood. The drawing by George Grosz is reproduced by the permission of the Estate of George Grosz, Princeton, New Jersey.

Contents

The Author

Dennis Davison, Litt.B., M.A., Ph.D., is Senior Lecturer in English at Monash University, Melbourne, Australia, and is the author of *Dryden* in this series.

I

Poet and Period

The first half of the 20th century must already have the quaint, dusty appearance of a remote historical period for young readers today, even though one of its celebrated literary figures is a living, potent voice, speaking directly to each individual in the unique way that poetry still insists on doing in an age of depersonalised mass-communication. Auden continues with his prolific output of reviews, essays, articles, lectures, translations, operatic libretti, anthologies, and editorial work, for he has wholeheartedly accepted the modern apparatus of cultural dissemination, and yet we return to his *poetry* for the most personal and intimate contact with a mind we respect, with a creative talent that never fails to captivate and surprise us.

As literary critics we approach with our box of adhesive labels and the first one we shall attempt to stick, like Dewey-Decimal digits, to his spine is: *Post 1918/Middle-Class*. And so we might begin by recalling the post-First World War age, in which Wystan Hugh Auden grew to manhood, and sketch the external biographical landmarks: for the inner landmarks we have to consult the poems themselves.

Auden was born in York on 21 February 1907. His mother had been a nurse and his father was a doctor. In 1908 the Auden family settled in Birmingham and Dr. Auden became Medical Officer and Professor of Public Health in Birmingham University. The home atmosphere was scientific, the library full of books on geology and machines, and Auden's intention was to become a mining engineer. He went to 'prep-school' (St. Edmund's) in 1915 where he met Christopher Isherwood, three years older than himself, and from 1920 to 1925 he was in Norfolk (at

Gresham's School, Holt) where he specialised in biology. Auden later recalled his schooldays in this way: 'The son of book-loving, Anglo-Catholic parents of the professional class . . . I was . . . mentally precocious, physically backward, short-sighted, a rabbit at all games, very untidy and grubby, a nail-biter, a physical coward, dishonest, sentimental, with no community sense whatever, in fact a typical little highbrow and difficult child.' His discovery of his vocation as a poet came to him at half-past three one afternoon in March 1922, as he walked across a ploughed field with a friend, and he published his first poem in 1924 in *Public School Verse*.

Auden was at Christ Church, Oxford, from 1925 to 1928. His tutor was Nevill Coghill (of Exeter College), and Auden responded to the impact of Old English verse as well as the provocatively modern poems of T. S. Eliot. The three years at Oxford now appear somewhat legendary to literary historians who speak of the Auden–Spender–Day-Lewis–Isherwood Oxford Period. Spender's account, in his autobiographical *World Within World*, and Day-Lewis's in *The Buried Day*, reveal how Auden impressed his fellow-students, but we should remember that in fact Day-Lewis was in his final year when he met Auden, who himself left a year ahead of Spender. Isherwood, of course, was at Cambridge but made visits to Auden's room to discuss literature. Seemingly Auden at this time read a good deal of psychology, analysed and advised his friends, and conceived the poet as a detached, clinical analyst of men and society, diagnosing individual or social ills, and applying poetry to them as a sort of psychological therapy. His friends pictured him, striding past the gasworks in a black frock-coat and carrying a starting-pistol, as a peculiar amalgam of mental surgeon, witchdoctor and buffoon. Theatrical poses are not unknown among under-graduates but Auden's 'fantasy-life' seems to have included a generous element of deliberate clowning.

Auden's first volume of poems, dedicated to Isherwood, was hand-printed by Stephen Spender at Oxford in 1928, and among imitations of Hopkins, and the familiar 'Taller to-day, we remember similar evenings', we find unromantic descriptive passages:

> Snatches of tramline running to the wood,
> An industry already comatose,
> Yet sparsely living. A ramshackle engine
> At Cashwell raises water; for ten years
> It lay in flooded workings. . . .

The urgent, clinical, enigmatic style of the early Auden is already formed, as we see in this untitled poem which was not reprinted later, though Auden salvaged the last line for another occasion:

> Consider if you will how lovers stand
> In brief adherence, straining to preserve
> Too long the suction of good-bye: others,
> Less clinically-minded, will admire
> An evening like a coloured photograph,
> A music stultified across the water.
> The desert opens here, and if, though we
> Have ligatured the ends of a farewell,
> Sporadic heartburn show in evidence
> Of love uneconomically slain,
> It is for the last time, the last look back,
> The heel upon the finishing blade of grass,
> To dazzling cities of the plain where lust
> Threatened a sinister rod, and we shall turn
> To our study of stones, to split Eve's apple,
> Absorbed, content if we can say 'because':
> Unanswerable like any other pedant,
> Like Solomon and Sheba, wrong for years.

After Oxford Auden spent a year (1928–9) in Berlin. Auden tells us that his parents offered him a year abroad and he un-expectedly chose Germany. ('For the generation of intellectuals immediately preceding mine, the only culture that counted was French culture. I was bored with hearing about it . . . Where then? Rome? No; Mussolini and Fascism made that impossible.') Here he came into contact with German cabaret-songs, Rilke's poetry, the theatre of Brecht, and the psychological ideas of John Layard (based on Freud and Groddeck but more immediately from Homer Lane). In March 1929 Isherwood joined Auden in Berlin.

From 1930–5 Auden, like many middle-class writers of his generation, was a schoolmaster (first in Scotland and then near Malvern) and while at these provincial private schools he published his early work which began to make a stir among the reading public of the Thirties. *Paid on Both Sides* and *Poems* were published in 1930, *The Orators* in 1932, *The Dance of Death* in 1933, written for the Group Theatre with which Auden was associated from 1932. In 1935 he collaborated with Isherwood on the play *The Dog Beneath the Skin* for the Group Theatre's first season in London (at Westminster Theatre) and also worked with the GPO Film Unit, together with Benjamin Britten. Already we note how Auden is in contact with leading writers and musicians, and a great deal of his entire output is a result of collaboration. Another feature of Auden's literary life is his visits to foreign countries. The stay in Germany is now followed by a trip to Iceland (July–September 1936) with another Birmingham schoolmaster-poet, Louis MacNeice, with whom he wrote *Letters from Iceland*, 1937. (This volume contains Auden's remarkable imitation of Byron's style in 'Letter to Lord Byron', an amusing and revealing commentary on himself and the current scene.) 1936 also saw the production of *The Ascent of F6*, Auden's best-known play, written with Isherwood, and the publication of a new volume of poems, *Look, Stranger!* (entitled *On This Island* in the American edition). It was dedicated to Erika Mann, daughter of the celebrated German novelist Thomas Mann; Auden had married her to provide her with a passport to enter England. In 1937, January–March, he made a visit to war-torn Spain and published his poem 'Spain': in 1938 he went to China with Isherwood (see *Journey to a War*, 1939). They travelled by way of the United States and, says John Lehmann, both decided during this trip to return and settle in America—a decision which caused left-wing circles to accuse them of abandoning the European political struggle with which they had been identified. *On the Frontier*, written with Isherwood, was produced this same year and is their most explicit political play. As a sidelight on Auden's unusual (and, to many, bewildering) versatility we might mention that in 1938 he also edited *The Oxford Book of Light*

Verse. What, demands an imaginary biographer, is happening in the mind of a poet who in one single year visits China, decides to live in America, writes a left-wing play, and edits light verse? The answer seems to be—becoming an Anglo-Catholic. (All of which illustrates the difficulty of gauging the inner development of a poet from a few known external facts.) Auden left England on 18 January 1939 for the United States, becoming an American citizen in 1946, and eventually made public his acceptance of Christianity. In America Auden continued to teach in various schools and universities and to give public lectures. From 1948 onwards he began to spend part of each year on the Italian island of Ischia but in 1957 he bought a farmhouse in Kirchstetten, Lower Austria, for spring and summer residence. He has been awarded numerous prizes and honours (King's Gold Medal, Guggenheim Fellowships, Pulitzer Prize, Bollingen Prize, National Book Award, Feltrinelli Prize) and was elected to the American Academy, to a fellowship at Christ Church, and to the Professorship of Poetry at Oxford University (1956–61). Since his residence in America he has accomplished an enormous amount of varied literary work, collaborating frequently with writers and composers, and has published an imposing amount of verse: *New Year Letter* (1941), *For the Time Being* (1944), *Collected Poetry* (1945), *The Age of Anxiety* (1947), *Collected Shorter Poems 1930–1944* (1950), *Nones* (1951), *The Shield of Achilles* (1955), *The Old Man's Road* (1956), *Selected Poetry* (1958), *Homage to Clio* (1960), *About the House* (1966), *Collected Longer Poems* (1968). His selected essays were printed in *The Dyer's Hand* (1962) and his lectures at the University of Kent appeared as *Secondary Worlds* (1968). In particular Auden has turned to music and opera as fields for collaboration, and shares in such work as *Hymn to St. Cecilia* (with Britten); *The Rake's Progress* (with Stravinsky); *Delia* (a libretto); English versions of Mozart's *The Magic Flute* and *Don Giovanni*, and of Brecht's *The Seven Deadly Sins*; Henze's opera *Elegy for Young Lovers*.

Merely to list Auden's multifarious literary works is now a task for a bibliographer, and the breadth of his interests might be suggested by a random choice of a few people he has written about, edited, translated, or reviewed: Skelton, Pope, Rilke, Thurber, Niehbuhr, Freud, Kipling, Kierkegaard, Kafka, Betjeman, Baudelaire, Dante, D. H. Lawrence, Henry James, Cervantes, Somerset Maugham, Poe, Colette, Virgil, Shakespeare, Cocteau, Lewis Carroll, Van Gogh, Cavafy, Dag Hammarskjöld, Goethe . . .

Despite Auden's reputation as the poetic voice of the Thirties, as the analyst of men and society, it is surprising how few topical references there are in his poems, though it may be that some of them we don't now recognise as immediately as his original readers would have. (For example: when we read of the Devil that 'like influenza he walks abroad' we probably don't recall the post-war epidemics—in 1918 there were 150,000 deaths in Britain. Or again, in the early poem quoted above, just how novel would a 'coloured photograph' be in 1928?) And so a very brief glance at the earlier part of this century might enable us to see Auden in the context of his times.

THE CONTEMPORARY SCENE

The political picture after the First World War is of nearly twenty years of Conservative power, together with the rising challenge of the Trade Union and Socialist movements. After the war there was an official Labour opposition, the Labour Party and the Trades Union Congress were reorganised, the *Daily Herald* (Labour's main organ of publicity) resumed daily publication, the Communist Party was formed in 1920, women (of thirty and over) had the right to vote, and in 1924 and 1929 there were two short-lived Labour governments under Ramsay MacDonald. After a brief post-war boom, inflation followed, with strikes and threatened strikes—in 1919 a police strike, in 1920 a railway strike, and in this same year the London dockers refused to load munitions on to the *Jolly George*, destined for the interventionist armies against Bolshevism in Russia. The 1921 slump, when 2,170,000 were unemployed, brought in the 'dole' system, but the basic economic problems, manifested to the general public in high prices and the acute housing shortage, were not solved. In 1926 came the General Strike, which lasted nine days (Auden was at Oxford by this time), and in 1929 the Wall Street crash. In 1920 there was civil war in Ireland: in 1922 Gandhi was sentenced to six years' gaol and a decade of riots and strikes followed in India. There were similar signs in Palestine and Egypt that the British Empire was to disappear. Fascism had already appeared on the horizon: in 1923 Mussolini sent warships to bombard Corfu.

A rapid survey of the period indicates the fundamental changes which were violently occurring in English society as working-class movements strove to replace rule by Conservative 'public-school boys' and businessmen. Population moved from depressed areas to London and the Home Counties, and other features of the times were: ribbon development of housing, giant industries (Portland cement, Shell oil, Courtauld's, Austin and Morris car manufacture, ICI, Unilever), Woolworth's stores, hire-purchase systems, the BBC (formed in 1922), and Yellow Press scandal-sheet journalism. Mass-society seemed to have arrived, not only with mass-production of buses, vans, lorries, cars and motor-cycles, or mass-circulation newspapers, but also with mass entertainments such as football, wrestling, dog-racing, and cinemas (there were 3,000 in 1929 when 'talkies' first appeared). In a period of chronic unemployment and economic crisis, true advances in personal liberty (such as the emancipation of women) were often mixed confusedly with passing phases of frivolity, escapist entertainment, and shallow crazes for novel ideas. Women wore shorter skirts and were openly indulging in drink, tobacco and cosmetics. Noël Coward's 'bright young things' or the new, voting 'flappers' made the headlines in the scandal-press, and the 'modern' note was struck by such varied things as cocktails, talkies, jazz, easier divorce, birth-control, radio, Freudian psychology, air-travel, a decline in churchgoing. The Twenties saw a reflection of both the frivolous and the serious social changes in the literature of the period—the sex-studies of Havelock Ellis, the novels of Aldous Huxley and D. H. Lawrence, Joyce's *Ulysses* (1922), Eliot's *The Waste Land* (1922), the 'Bloomsbury Group' and Virginia Woolf (*Mrs. Dalloway*, 1925), Galsworthy's *Forsyte Saga* (1922), the prolific works of

Shaw and H. G. Wells, Forster's *Passage to India* (1924), and the spate of anti-war war books. One should also mention the scientific field: in 1919 there is Rutherford's account of splitting the atom, and the confirmation of Einstein's theories of relativity and the space–time continuum. There is also great progress in genetics, but to most people the remarkable advances in technology (cars, airplanes, cinema, radio, industrial engineering) would have been more evident.

The Thirties saw an increase in tension. The Wall Street crash of 1929 heralded the Great World Depression of 1929–32, with six million unemployed in Germany in 1932 and three and three-quarter million in England, i.e. some six to seven million people living on the dole. The General Strike of 1926 had demonstrated that Socialism could not be achieved merely by a spectacular act of workers' solidarity, and the formation of a national government in 1931 (when MacDonald joined Baldwin and Chamberlain and 'betrayed' socialism) led many left-wingers to place their hopes in Communism. The Soviet Union was now facing a Fascist Italy and a resurgent Nazi Germany, and in 1936 the ideological conflict was to become a real battleground in Spain (which Auden visited in 1937). In 1932 the British Union of Fascists was formed, and there was a notoriously brutal mass rally of Fascists at Olympia in 1934. (Mosley, the leader of the BUF, was still travelling the world to promote his cause in 1969.) In March 1936 Hitler reoccupied the Rhineland; in May 1936 the Italians captured the capital of Abyssinia; in July 1937 Japan began an undeclared war on China; in March 1938 Hitler's troops occupied Vienna; between autumn 1938 and March 1939 Germany completed the conquest of Czechoslovakia, negotiated at Munich by Hitler, Mussolini, Daladier and Chamberlain. A few months later, in September 1939, the Second World War began. Auden had left for America in January 1939, after Hitler's first steps towards the subjection of the Czechs.

The paradox of the Twenties and Thirties is that in many ways life became easier and more varied for most sections of the population because of technological advances and mass-production, while at the same time fundamental economic crises

16

led to a permanent pool of unemployment, and class bitterness was intense. For Auden, educated at public school and university, a member of the professional middle classes, there was the reasonably secure position as schoolmaster and a certain amount of paid work in the commercial literary field. Presumably his contact with working-class life—the factories, the squalid slums or the new Council houses, weekends in Youth Hostels at a shilling a night or the yearly holiday at a Butlin holiday-camp, dog-racing, Saturday football-watching, the corner pub, Woolworth's, the local cinema or dance-hall, the public library, the dole—would be small, as would be his first-hand knowledge of business circles or London high society. Poets have in the past been courtiers or Grub Street hacks; dependent on wealthy patrons or publishers or the Globe Theatre receipts; but typically the modern poet chooses teaching as a profession (as the 18th-century poet chose the Church) or else survives on the fringe of the literary industry as reviewer, editor or detective-story writer. He is a minor part of the middle-class scene; a worker, but rarely on the dole; sharing middle-class cultural privileges but with neither the wealth nor the power of the ruling *élite*. He is not in an ideal central position so much as torn between two worlds, neither of which he knows well nor can identify himself with. It can be a state of isolation, of uncertain allegiances, of wavering sympathies. (Auden alternates between indignation at working-class conditions and disgust at working-class apathy.) The writers of the Thirties were aware of the existence of 'two nations'. In J. B. Priestley's *English Journey* (1934) one could visit comfortable suburbia; in Walter Greenwood's *Love on the Dole* (1933) or George Orwell's *The Road to Wigan Pier* (1937) one was confronted with the bitter conditions of the poor. But if large audiences were applauding Noël Coward's patriotic *Cavalcade* at Drury Lane in 1931, others were reading the *New Statesman*, *Left Review*, the cheap volumes from the Left Book Club, and the writings of G. D. H. Cole, Harold Laski, Raymond Postgate, Shaw, Wells and Priestley. How far these currents were mirrored in the other arts is hard to say, but the Thirties were not barren of significant creative work: the functional architecture connected with E. Maxwell Fry, the large-scale sculptures of Jacob Epstein, the fine carving of Eric Gill, the puzzling simplicity of Henry Moore, the mixture of traditionalism and modernity in the music of Ralph Vaughan Williams.

Rightly or wrongly, for most readers Auden, Spender, Day-Lewis, Isherwood and MacNeice are regarded as the significant figures of the Thirties, and in particular the first three have been linked together and identified with left-wing poetry. As Alan Ross says in his British Council pamphlet *Poetry 1945–1950*: 'The most arresting poetry of the Thirties, that written by W. H. Auden, Stephen Spender, Louis MacNeice and C. Day-Lewis, reflected two main preoccupations: a growing concern about the class structure, based on a Marxist analysis of capitalist society, and an awareness of the inevitability of a European war ... The poetic movement of the Thirties acted as the decade's moral conscience.' Alan Ross, writing in 1951, adds that the Auden-led movement disintegrated when the war began, for Auden 'the symbolic figurehead . . . abdicated just before the war, the throne fell and has not been occupied since'.

THE REVOLUTIONARY'S PROGRESS

Critics have not been slow to note that the left-wing, middle-class protesters of the Thirties, for whom bourgeois society was decadent and ripe for overthrowing, have found comfortable niches for themselves in that society, accepted its honours, and joined its church. As J. M. Cohen, in *Poetry of This Age*, says of Auden: 'The protest is over ... the poetry is to this day muddled in its statements, clever in its acrobatic off-beat rhythms, and ultimately defeatist. The poet has taken refuge on an island of intellectualism from which he fervently proclaims in the most intellectual of language that intellectualism is a barren pursuit.' Others have commented ironically that Comrade Day-Lewis (who, like Spender, was a member of the Communist Party) should become a CBE, an Anglican, Professor of Poetry at Oxford, and Poet Laureate: that Comrade Spender, CBE, is now a respectable literary editor and visiting university professor: that, of other poets associated with the Auden group, Charles Madge is Professor of Sociology at Birmingham, Rex Warner is Professor of Classics at the University of Connecticut, and Louis MacNeice became a successful writer for the BBC. Auden, of course, is regarded as the arch-convert to the bourgeois establishment—American citizen, Anglo-Catholic, professor-at-large in England and America, and recipient of many honours and prizes. A pointer to Auden's changed political views is seen in a letter (reprinted in *The Age*, Melbourne, 30 December 1967) about the Vietnam War. The poet who had supported the left wing in Spain in 1937 wrote thirty years later: 'But what do I, or any other writer in the West, know about Vietnam, except what we can glean from the newspapers and a few hurriedly written books? . . . I believe a negotiated peace, to which the Viet Cong will have to be a party, to be possible, but not yet, and that, therefore, American troops, alas, must stay in Vietnam until it is. But it would be absurd to call this answer mine. It simply means that I am an American citizen who reads *The New York Times*.'

Is the pattern of *youthful protest: middle-aged conformism* inevitable for the middle-class poet? The 20th-century attraction to and reaction against the Russian Revolution is rather similar to the changes in attitude among the Romantic poets to the French Revolution. Here is the young Wordsworth speaking of his radical views (in *The Prelude*, IX, 518–32):

> . . . I with him believed
> That a benignant spirit was abroad
> Which might not be withstood, that poverty
> Abject as this would in a little time
> Be found no more, that we should see the earth
> Unthwarted in her wish to recompense
> The meek, the lowly, patient child of toil,
> All institutes for ever blotted out
> That legalised exclusion, empty pomp
> Abolished, sensual state and cruel power,
> Whether by edict of the one or few;

And finally, as sum and crown of all,
Should see the people having a strong hand
In framing their own laws; whence better days
To all mankind. . . .

Yet in 1832, in the sonnet 'Upon the Late General Fast', Wordsworth, now 62, hopes that the people will seek help from God against 'the pestilence of revolution'. The young Coleridge, in his 'Destruction of the Bastile', spoke in these exultant tones:

I see, I see! glad Liberty succeed
With every patriot virtue in her train!
And mark yon peasant's raptur'd eyes;
Secure he views his harvests rise;
No fetter vile the mind shall know,
And Eloquence shall fearless glow.
Yes! Liberty the Soul of Life shall reign,
Shall throb in every pulse, shall flow thro' every vein!

He later became disillusioned with the Revolution and adopted conservative philosophical and religious views. Byron and Shelley did not survive long enough to manifest any such changes of attitude, but they have left us testimony of their radicalism. When the Nottingham weavers smashed machine looms Byron defended them in these sympathetic lines of satire against the mill-owners:

O well done Lord Eldon and better done Ryder,
Britannia must prosper with councils like yours;
Hawkesby, Harrowby, help you to guide her,
Whose remedy only must *kill* ere it cures:
Those villains, the weavers, are all grown refractory,
Asking some succour for Charity's sake—
So hang them in clusters round each Manufactory,
That will at once put an end to *mistake*.

The rascals, perhaps, might betake them to robbing,
The dogs to be sure have got nothing to eat—
So if we hang them for breaking a bobbin,
'Twill save all the Government's money and meat.

Men are more easily made than machinery—
Stockings fetch better prices than lives—
Gibbets on Sherwood will heighten the scenery,
Shewing how Commerce, how Liberty thrives.

(It is interesting to see Byron, whom Auden admires and imitates, using a ballad style for public satire just as Auden is to turn to popular song for his social commentary verse.) Shelley's hatred of political and religious tyranny is intense; in his 'Ode to Liberty' he exhorts free men to 'stamp the impious name/Of KING into the dust' and hopes that 'the pale name of PRIEST might shrink and dwindle/Into the hell from which it first was hurled . . .' In 'The Mask of Anarchy', written after the 'massacre' of workers at Manchester, he urges the poor to revolt against the rich:

Rise like Lions after slumber
In unvanquishable number,
Shake your chains to earth like dew
Which in sleep had fallen on you—
Ye are many—they are few.

This glimpse of an earlier generation of middle- and upper-class poets (and there are other examples in the Romantic period) should make us less surprised at Auden and his contemporaries, who have moved from protest to relative acquiescence. One must frankly admit that Auden, Spender and Day-Lewis have abandoned their left-wing criticism of bourgeois society: they have become successful, middle-class poets writing for their own class. Could one really have expected otherwise? For one thing, the poet must live and so must either sell enough of his poetry on the market or obtain a job that affords leisure to write; so in one way or another he compromises with the society he perhaps despises. For another thing, the political situation today has also changed from that of the Thirties: some left-wing poets may now feel that bourgeois society has itself swung leftwards (partly as a result of their protest verse) and that, as communism is also developing distinct forms in different countries, the struggle of Left versus Right is much more complex. I am not sure how valid these arguments are. I have my own prejudices, of course; I admire Shaw for not accepting any honours from the society he attacked, and Sean O'Casey for remaining a working-class writer, describing the life of the class he knew at first hand. The poet who has opinions (whatever they are) on the Vietnam War, the quality of life in the British 'Welfare State', racial tension in America, peasant life in Argentina, student protests, controversy within the Catholic Church, sexual inequality in Australia, permissive morality, concentration camps, space travel—to cite a random list of topical questions—does not need to have any particular ideological commitment, but he will be contributing to our awareness and understanding of the world we have to come to terms with. When the middle-class poet—be he Shakespeare, Goethe or T. S. Eliot—interests himself in the significant features of his own times he can command our attention, whether we agree with him or not. *The Canterbury Tales*, *The Faerie Queene* and *Paradise Lost* dealt with important aspects of the times in which they were written; a great deal remains of interest (though we are not so immediately concerned today with, for example, pilgrimages, or the chivalric code, or Milton's discussion of the digestive system of angels). One of the paradoxes of literature is that a writer with a conservative outlook can produce work that will be acclaimed by progressives: one recalls that Karl Marx praised highly the 'reactionary' novelist Balzac and declared that the literature of Ancient Greece, a class society based on slavery, had never been surpassed. And so, as we look at the evolving work of W. H. Auden, *Post-1918/Middle-Class*, we shall try to see how period and class limited or aided his vision, and to what extent his poetry achieves a relevance beyond its origin in time or society.

2

Poet of the Thirties

For many people today Auden is still the outstanding poet of the Thirties. He is a reputation, a myth, even a period-piece, rather than a living poet who is still writing. In 1967 the BBC broadcast a tribute to Auden on his sixtieth birthday and most of the poems quoted were Thirties poems, some of which Auden has long since dismissed as shameful rubbish. One quip in the programme seemed to crystallise the underlying feeling that the dynamic young poet had turned into a tourist's curio as, speaking of Auden's deeply-furrowed face, one person commented: 'He left for America looking like a Boy Scout and he's returned looking like a Red Indian squaw.'

Early photographs of Auden show him as blond, lean-jawed, alert, urgent, as he smokes a cigarette and looks fearlessly into the future—or is it only into the camera? The shot is carefully posed: one suspects the subject is also. At any rate, Auden seems to have impressed his undergraduate friends and fellow-writers by his self-assurance, his erudition, his aura of mysterious powers. Looking back at a meeting with Auden and Isherwood, in his autobiography *World Within World*, Stephen Spender can now view the scene rather sardonically:

> Our first meeting was in Auden's rooms on a bright sunny afternoon. As Auden hated the daylight, all the blinds were drawn and the electric light was on. Seated at a table covered with manuscripts were Auden and Isherwood. Auden wore a green shade over his eyes, and looked like an amateur chemist. Isherwood looked like a schoolboy playing charades. The manuscripts were their respective books. Auden looked up abruptly when I came in and said: 'You're early. Sit down.' Isherwood giggled, and while I sat

down he turned to Auden and said: 'But really I don't see the image of a "frozen gull flipped down the weir": it sounds like cold storage.' Auden flushed and struck out the lines with a thick lead pencil.

p. 88

The literary climate of the Thirties was largely established by the flurry of magazines and anthologies which not only presented new poems, stories and plays but which encouraged personal attacks and ripostes in an atmosphere of literary guerrilla warfare. Michael Roberts, for instance, was responsible for *New Signatures* (1932), the fiercely propagandist collection *New Country* (1933), and *The Faber Book of Modern Verse* (1936). Other *avant-garde* journals were *Contemporary Poetry and Prose*, with its insistent political stress, Julian Symons's *Twentieth Century Verse*, and, perhaps the most influential, *New Verse*, edited by the sharp-tongued Geoffrey Grigson (with the help, later, of Kenneth Allott). Rather different in tone was F. R. Leavis's *Scrutiny* which praised and castigated writers with dry, donnish phrases. Although *New Verse*'s favourite target was Edith Sitwell, who was pictured as aristocratic, eccentric and conceited, it also kept a close watch on its favoured sons. Auden was criticised for accepting the King's Medal, Pound, Eliot and Herbert Read for sympathy with Social Credit theories, and C. Day-Lewis for acting as selector for the Book Society. Grigson's pungent comments on this backsliding by one of the most vocal anti-bourgeois poets give us a glimpse of the intensity of the literary-political life of the times:

The Book Society is a Limited Company pimping to the mass *bourgeois* mind and employing 'distinguished' members of the literary underworld, *adopters* of literature as a profession, writers each of no more real existence than a tick lost in the last five minutes of a cuckoo clock. On this Committee, Mr. Day Lewis no doubt will be Change, Revolution, Youth, the Rising Generation. But this ends his stance as the Poet writing thrillers . . . and establishes him as the Thriller Writer, the Underworld Man, the yesterday's newspaper, the grease in the sink-pipe of letters . . . Mr. Day Lewis and his Legend are now liquidated: the liquid has flowed to its oily shape and low level in the old sardine tin of Respectability. Mr. Lewis has drained himself off, a Noyes, a Binyon, a Squire, a dullard.

We can get along without him.

No doubt—to imitate Grigson's mixed metaphors—the Book Society was the thin end of the wedge opening the sardine tin of Respectability. The present Mr. C. Day-Lewis (he now hyphenates his names) CBE, became an Anglican, and Poet Laureate, and features in *Who's Who*. This indeed is the story of many of the rebels of the Thirties: they have accepted, and been accepted by, the Establishment, decorated with honours, appointed to university chairs or directorships of respectable publishing firms. Auden's honours, as listed in *Who's Who*, would be enough to make a dozen poets contented.

At first the Thirties poets looked with admiration to earlier writers who had established modern poetry—Hardy, Yeats, Eliot, Pound and Graves. The contemporary reader must have had a fairly confused impression of new trends, represented as they were by such different writers as Auden, Empson, John Betjeman, Dylan Thomas, Anne Ridler, George Barker, Roy Fuller and D. H. Lawrence (to mention but a few), and it soon became clear that the identification disc round the neck of a Genuine Thirties Poet said plainly 'Left-Wing Revolutionary'. Political allegiance of the wrong kind now damned a poet in the eyes of the critics. Yeats, Pound and Eliot were all attracted, to different degrees, to the ideas of Mussolini, and when Eliot visited Fascist Portugal at least one man wrote a bitterly witty poem lamenting the lost leader.

Before we look at Auden's left-wing poems of this period we might glance at those of some of his contemporaries to see Auden's work in perspective. And we immediately find that the militant, optimistic note of political revolution is struck most forcefully by Cecil Day-Lewis, Auden's friend at Oxford. In E. Allen Osborne's volume of anti-Fascist writings, called appropriately *In Letters of Red* (1938), appeared Day-Lewis's 'On the Twentieth Anniversary of Soviet Power', of which this is a typical passage:

Twenty years have passed
Since a cry, All Power to the Soviets! shook the world.
We have seen new cities, arts and sciences,
A real freedom, a justice that flouts not nature,
Springing like corn exuberant from the rich heart
Of a happier people. We have seen their hope take off
From solid ground and confidently fly
Out to the mineral north, the unmapped future.
U.S.S.R.! The workers of every land
And all who believe man's virtue inexhaustible
Greet you to-day: you are their health, their home,
The vision's proof, the lifting of despair.
Red Star, be steadfast above this treacherous age!
We look to you, we salute you.

In this same volume Auden was represented by 'Dover', which
may not strike us now as a particularly political poem, but which
presumably seemed more pointed to contemporary readers.
Dover, the port which traditionally links England with Europe,
is presented as non-productive (there are no industries), as a
somewhat seedy snob resort for the rich, the point of departure
for migrants, the pleasure-ground of soldiers—the lighthouse is
'ruined', the sea-front is 'almost elegant' and 'Nothing is made
in this town.' It is a town of bureaucrats and experts, of the
lonely who each egotistically 'prays in the dusk for himself',
and of soldiers as frivolous as middle-class schoolgirls. One
stanza will show how Auden produces his laconic, critical snapshots by the juxtaposition of revealing details and ironical
comments:

The soldiers swarm in the pubs in their pretty clothes,
As fresh and silly as girls from a high-class academy.
The Lion, the Rose, the Crown will not ask them to die,
Not now, not here. All they are killing is time,
    Their pauper civilian future.

Without any strident appeals or denunciations Auden handles
this low-keyed conversational style which disarmingly insists
on the decadence of the old order—its nostalgic Georgian houses,
its vanishing elegance, its economic stagnation, its middle-class

education, its musical-comedy soldiery. What the decadent bourgeoisie is unaware of is the ominous political future for an England no longer a safe island-fortress:

> Above them, expensive and lovely as a rich child's toy,
> The aeroplanes fly in the new European air,
> On the edge of that air that makes England of little importance . . .

Beyond the political menace is the inevitable cosmic doom. Scientists were making men aware that the sun was a cooling star—a salutary thought for the sunbather on the Dover beaches:

> And the tides warn bronzing bathers of a cooling star
> With half its history done.

This poem is not a bitter attack on the 'system', not an optimistic shout to a socialist future, but a left-wing lament. The detached observer finishes with a wry shrug of the shoulders:

> And the cry of the gulls at dawn is sad like work.
> . . . Some are temporary heroes.
> Some of these people are happy.

C. Day-Lewis of course has other moods and styles than those seen in his tribute to the Soviet Union. His long poem *The Magnetic Mountain*, dedicated to Auden, contains a rich variety of verses bound together by the central symbol of a train ride from the reactionary present to the ideal Communist mountain of the future. Sometimes his warnings and threats are couched in jaunty, joking style and there are chummy references to fellow-comrades, Wystan Auden and Rex Warner:

> Make no mistake, this is where you get off,
> Sue with her suckling, Cyril with his cough,
> Bert with a blazer and a safety-razor,
> Old John Braddleum and Terence the toff.
> And now, may I ask, have you made any plans?
> You can't go further along these lines;
> Positively this is the end of the track;
> It's rather late and there's no train back . . .
> Then book your bed-sitter at the station hotel,
> Or stay at the terminus till you grow verminous,

> Eating chocolate creams from the slot-machines;
> But don't blame me when you feel unwell . . .
> Then I'll hit the trail for that promising land;
> May catch up with Wystan and Rex my friend,
> Go mad in good company, find a good country,
> Make a clean sweep or make a clean end.

Auden's first volume, *Poems* (1930), also contains a versatile variety of poems, and number XXII, beginning 'Get there if you can', reminds us of Day-Lewis's lines with their everyday imagery and crisp condemnation of England in decay, though Auden's angry accusations are found side by side with grim catalogues of a run-down economy:

> Smokeless chimneys, damaged bridges, rotting wharves
>   and choked canals,
> Tramlines buckled, smashed trucks lying on their side
>   across the rails . . .

3–4

These laconic details are more telling perhaps than the ironic picture of the wealthy friends who betray:

> At the theatre, playing tennis, driving motor cars we had,
> In our continental villas, mixing cocktails for a cad.
> These were boon companions who devised their legends for our
>   tombs,
> These who have betrayed us nicely while we took them to our
>   rooms.

15–18

The stanzas move from topic to topic with a disconcerting lack of connections. At one moment we are having a seaside holiday on 'the sopping esplanade', but this image is followed by a comment on the cultural heroes 'once healers in our English land':

> Lawrence was brought down by smut-hounds, Blake went dotty
>   as he sang,
> Homer Lane was killed in action by the Twickenham Baptist gang.

37–8

After more disjointed stanzas, with obscurely ominous hints of factory girls destroying intellectuals, the poem ends with what seems to be a final warning to the bourgeoisie to really change itself or die:

> Drop those priggish ways for ever, stop behaving like a stone:
> Throw the bath-chairs right away, and learn to leave ourselves
>   alone.
> If we really want to live, we'd better start at once to try;
> If we don't, it doesn't matter, but we'd better start to die.

51–4

Here Auden, like T. S. Eliot in *The Waste Land*, presents his ideas through a series of apparently unrelated images, instead of selecting a well-defined target and aiming accusations at it with methodical argument and observable logic. There is a certain loss in clarity, a certain mystification even, though like his fellow revolutionary poets Auden does seem to accept the basic notion that society must change or die. But although various social, or class, changes are envisaged it is significant that Auden is asking for a 'change of heart', not a change of conditions, and that he thinks the middle classes (including himself perhaps) are worth changing. In other words, this is not a proletarian poem, urging the workers to organise a revolution, but an appeal from a disillusioned bourgeois to his own class. In 1955 (in 'Authority In America', *The Griffin*) Auden recognised this: 'Looking back, it seems to me that the interest in Marx taken by myself and my friends . . . was more psychological than political; we were interested in Marx in the same way that we were interested in Freud, as a technique of unmasking middle-class ideologies, not with the intention of repudiating our class, but with the hope of becoming better bourgeois . . .'

Not that the oblique approach to politics is peculiar to Auden. I imagine that all poets try to avoid the crude didactic ways of propaganda literature and its hurrah-for-us-to-hell-with-them harangues, appeals and denunciations. One has only to remember Dryden to see how the more indirect satire and allegory can be employed for partisan verse, and in the 1930s these traditional methods were probably encouraged by techniques made popular by the surrealist movement. André Breton, its leader, made it clear that surrealism went 'hand in hand with the interests of the working class', though it is open to doubt whether the working class has ever felt like going hand in hand with the surrealists. But some of their devices, such as the incoherent logic of dreams, the humour of absurdity, shocking juxtapositions of unlikely objects, or terrifying symbols of space and time, were borrowed by poets from the painters. Louis MacNeice in his much-anthologised 'Bagpipe Music' (1938) presents a hilarious set of images of the times; zany stanzas are found cheek by jowl with ironic comments on unemployment, elections and middle-class status symbols ('Their knickers are made of crêpe-de-chine, their shoes are made of python'). If this following stanza is meant to be an exposition of ruling-class incompetence and working-class overpopulation problems, one can only say that the political message is submerged in music-hall guffaws:

> The Laird o' Phelps spent Hogmanay declaring he was sober,
> Counted his feet to prove the fact and found he had one foot over.
> Mrs. Carmichael had her fifth, looked at the job with repulsion,
> Said to the midwife 'Take it away; I'm through with over-
> production.'

George Barker's seemingly illogical patterns of whirling images, shocking visual details, and doom-filled warnings, may owe something to surrealist paintings and films—one remembers the screened shot of an eyeball slowly being cut by a razor-blade—but in 'Vision of England '38' the imagery is sometimes organised by the use of allegorical figures. Here for instance the poverty of Northern England (he alludes at one point to the closed shipyards at Jarrow) is pictured as a woman despoiled by her Southern lover:

> 'Yes, the South in his bowler and morning jacket,
> His leather satchel, and handkerchief in pocket,
> He called me a whore, but when he'd had his worth
> Not a penny he paid me for the child I bring forth.'

She ran her hand through her hair. I saw
Jarrow on her third finger like a lead ring.
'Yes', she said, 'he absconded after the war.
The husband for whom I wore flowers in the spring.

'Write it red in your lines, O write it red,
I starve with my children on the northern seaboard.
Warn well the pot-bellied and the over-fed,
I'll have their hearts to fill my echoing cupboard.'

Barker's 'South in his bowler' could be matched with Auden's
symbol for class privilege, the gamekeeper, which appears
threateningly at the end of poem xxv ('Who will endure'),
published in 1933. The poem itself is an evocation of inactivity
and crisis, in striking, concrete phrases ('Disaster stammered
over wires') although one is puzzled about the specific subject
of the poem. Does it describe a state of mind or the state of
England? And so the concluding lines may simply be taking
an image from the life of the land-owning class as a metaphor to
convey the limitations imposed upon a human mind:

For no one goes
Further than railhead or the ends of piers,
Will neither go nor send his son
Further through foothills than the rotting stack
Where gaitered gamekeeper with dog and gun
Will shout 'Turn back.'

Many of Auden's early poems, attractively employing images
from modern life, must have spoken with great impact to his
readers, but on reflection one is often unsure what they are really
about. Auden's habit of printing his verse without titles and
disregarding chronological order of composition leaves us without the usual guidelines which poets provide, and he has often
disconcerted critics by his custom of saving good lines or passages
from an abandoned work, in order to insert them in a later composition. This canny Yorkshire parsimony, it has been humorously
suggested, reveals that Auden is more concerned with the

success of local detail than with the impact of the poem as a whole. Spender has spoken of Auden's 'lack of the sense of the inner form of a poem'. It is as though Auden were a doctor, collecting evidence of the symptoms of the disease of modern civilisation, and displaying them in any suitable poem. In a sense, all the poems in the 1930 volume might just as well be seen as thirty sections of one long poem, diverse shots that together can be edited to make a film. The trouble is that the reader himself has to do the editing and find a title for the film. Is it Auden's version of *The Waste Land* or, as some suspect, a glimpse into a young man's contemplative but troubled mind?

Troubled but not confused. Many people have recalled the young Auden as a man of incisive counsel, a guide whose personal or literary advice was assured and compelling. Apparently, also, he enjoyed his years as a schoolmaster, and the schoolmasterly tone, of authority mingled with affection, has often been noticed in Auden's verse. Poem xxx ('Sir, no man's enemy . . .'), the last one in Auden's first published volume, has always enjoyed great popularity with readers and summarises in its fourteen lines Auden's position on many questions. It was later titled 'Petition', but it was excluded from the *Collected Shorter Poems 1927–1957* as being a 'dishonest poem', expressing a desire for 'New styles of architecture' though the author in fact prefers old styles.

The petition is addressed presumably to God, though the unusual 'Sir' (employed, incidentally, by Gerard Manley Hopkins) suggests a headmaster or a superior officer, and the poem succinctly lists the moral defects to be cured and the virtues to be encouraged. The old Christian labels for sins are replaced by a new phraseology from medicine and psychology—the 'neural itch', or the 'liar's quinsy', or the 'rehearsed response'. No doubt such phrases gave the poem a cold scientific glitter in 1930, an air of unsentimental analysis far removed from old-fashioned, Christian, breast-beating remorse. To ask God (rather peremptorily) to cure, prohibit, correct, publish, harrow and cover with a spotlight—to quote Auden's verbs of command—gives an impression of pertly instructing God on the necessary steps to be taken. 'Instructions' might be a more appropriate title than 'Petition'.

Auden's list of vices and virtues is interesting. The one unforgivable thing is the will's 'negative inversion', which seems a psychology text-book term for refusal to exercise free-will. What 'the intolerable neural itch' means precisely is not clear: perhaps neurosis. The 'exhaustion of weaning' alludes rather obscurely to a current psychological notion and the witty phrase 'the distortions of ingrown virginity' refers to the Freudian belief that sexual continence could lead to serious 'repressions'. Auden's technical vocabulary really springs from his belief at the time that diseases were caused by spiritual defects, and that sexual repression was a sin that caused disease of the body and mind. The optimistic second half of the poem assumes that cowardice can be corrected and those 'in retreat' be made to return with the aid of a powerful spotlight—perhaps the psychoanalyst's probing interrogation. 'Healers', a characteristic term for unorthodox doctors, perhaps psychiatrists, but suggesting 'faith-healers' and various biblical references to Christ, exist in cities, and God is to act almost as an advertiser for them. Finally God is bidden to '. . . look shining at/New styles of architecture, a change of heart'. The new experiments in starkly functional architecture and a new clinical attitude to life are juxtaposed with the provocative suggestion that one reflects the other.

One can imagine the novelty of this poem's language and tone for its contemporary readers. It borders on the insolent, it seems terribly up-to-date with its diagnoses and cures, it appears to be on the side of sex and the new architecture, it condemns some things sharply, but hopefully recommends willpower and a 'change of heart'. This final cliché seems sentimental and out of place, but somehow leaves one with the comforting impression that clinical young Mr. Auden is really a good, old-fashioned Christian under that white, surgical coat. (And some would add that his later conversion to Anglicanism has proved it.)

Thus, for all its modernity, this 'petition' to God, with its stress on moral correction and inner convictions, is not really very far from traditional religious attitudes. The novel vocabulary and the Freudian touches are to some extent removable camou-flage. If we compare this poem with one which was in fact called 'Instructions', we shall see that the *newness* which revolutionary poetry celebrated had usually an exhilaration, a naïvety, and an outward-looking character, which Auden's poem does not share:

> After the revolution, all that we have seen
> Flitting as shadows on the flatness of the screen
> Will stand out solid, will walk for all to touch
> For doubters to thrust hands in and cry, yes, it is such.
> . . . .
> Back of the streets and houses, back of all we had,
> Back of our rooms, furniture, systems, words said,
> The flow went on; we feel it now; the future was in our bones
> And it springs out, bursts in drums, trumpets and saxophones.
> . . . .
> It shines and we see it in the eyes and smiles of the stars,
> It laughs in the newspapers and underground, plays in the
>   headlights of cars . . .

So said Charles Madge in 1933. For him it is the social world, the solid world of objects, that will be transformed by revolution. In contrast to this, Auden's brief mention of 'New styles of architecture' seems a mere afterthought: his main concern is the inner transformation of man. (And presumably Charles Madge is still studying the social transformations of our period as Professor of Sociology at Birmingham University.)

In 1932, Auden published in *The Twentieth Century* magazine his most openly left-wing poem, 'A Communist to Others'. Spender has suggested that Auden was writing as though from the point of view of a Communist rather than in his own name, but it seems significant that in 1936 he deleted the title and six stanzas, altering the first word 'Comrades' to 'Brothers', and in 1945 suppressed the poem entirely. The speaker seems to be a middle-class intellectual addressing workers from 'office, shop and factory' on the need to co-operate against the common enemy. The language is simple and the speaker tries not to appear condescending:

> We cannot put on airs with you
> The fears that hurt you hurt us too . . .

The young bourgeois is addressed ironically:

> O splendid person, you who stand
> In spotless flannels or with hand
>   Expert on trigger;

but the future belongs to the workers whom the handsome young man regards as 'a nasty sight'. The Communist then attacks various types of people who delude the workers, such as the mystics who offer religion to the starving, the wise man who with detached humour diagnoses the workers' ills as 'lack of money', and the Cambridge liberals who prove that 'wealth and poverty are merely/Mental pictures'. On all these enemies the speaker heaps his curses:

> Let fever sweat them till they tremble,
> Cramp rack their limbs till they resemble
>   Cartoons by Goya . . .

The bourgeois' allies are listed fairly exhaustively—professors, agents, magic-makers, poets, apostles, bankers, brokers, club-room fossils—and in particular the 'Unhappy poet' is pictured as an escapist who 'fled in horror from all these/To islands in your private seas'. However, the Communist extends a comradely hand to the poet:

> You need us more than you suppose
> And you could help us if you chose.

The ending to this poem is puzzling. The workers are not exhorted to trust in their organised power, or in the inevitability of the historical process, but in love. And love is spoken of in terms which suggest a religious concept of a divine, unifying, protecting providence:

> Remember that in each direction
> Love outside our own election
> Holds us in unseen connection:
>   O trust that ever.

If this poem really represents Auden's commitment to communism it is very diappointing. Not only is the language an uneasy mixture of would-be simplicity, facile irony, forced abuse and misplaced jokiness ('You hide the boss's simple stuma/ Among the foes which we enumer'), but the speaker is obviously more at home verbally chastising the hunting-and-shooting set, mystics, Cambridge liberals, and escapist poets, than in understanding working-class life and its problems. Without wishing to, Auden has in fact demonstrated that the middle-class left-wing intellectual of the Thirties did find that, in practice, identification with the workers was immeasurably more difficult than writing a sympathetic poem to the revolution. Despite the example of middle-class intellectuals such as Marx and Lenin it remained almost impossible for bourgeois writers to write either for or about the working class. As the Marxist critic and poet, Christopher Caudwell, said in 1937: 'There is no classless art except communist art, and that is not yet born.' (*Illusion and Reality*, p. 288.) When Auden was revising his work for his *Collected Poetry* volume he wrote a comment about this poem in the book he was using as printer's copy. It reads: 'O God, what rubbish.'

Poem number XXIX ('Consider this and in our time'), later entitled 'Consider', comes to us with the highest recommendations from John Bayley, who, including Auden in his book significantly named *The Romantic Survival* (1957), calls it 'perhaps the finest poem' in the 1930 volume. But A. Alvarez, in *The Shaping Spirit* (1958), declares that 'Part of it has genius, part is hack-work.' Both critics note the contrast between the passages of detached, controlled description and the passages of sinister tension and horror, but whereas Bayley explains this by saying that 'Auden is describing present-day society as if it were seen by a schizophrenic,' Alvarez more disparagingly asserts that 'it has the air of having been written by two hands, the real poet and the hack . . . While either end of the poem is detached and deadly accurate, the central section is a blur of ominousness and threat, like a child telling a horror story; he manages to frighten himself without ever quite knowing what the horror is.' I allude to these two intelligent critics to show that a poem published in 1930 remains puzzling some thirty years later. Obscurity is hardly the most welcome feature in left-wing poetry aimed at spotlighting the class-enemy or enlightening progressives, and once more one wonders at Auden's reputation as a revolutionary poet in the Thirties. And yet Charles Madge in 1933 could record this kind of reaction to Auden's poems:

> But there waited for me in the summer morning,
> Auden, fiercely. I read, shuddered and knew
> And all the world's stationary things
> In silence moved to take up new positions . . .

The poem opens by asking us to consider bourgeois civilisation from a distance—'As the hawk sees it or the helmeted airman'—and, like a film camera panning a scene or approaching for a close-up, the poem presents us with varied shots of the rich at play. The camera pauses over the 'cigarette-end smouldering on a border' at a garden party, and then invites us to

> Pass on, admire the view of the massif
> Through plate-glass windows of the Sport Hotel,
> Join there the insufficient units
> Dangerous, easy, in furs, in uniform
> And constellated at reserved tables
> Supplied with feelings by an efficient band
> Relayed elsewhere to farmers and their dogs
> Sitting in kitchens in the stormy fens.

6–13

I think most readers will respond readily to this kind of verse, with its neatly-chosen detail, sophisticated nasty comments, and the overall condemnation of the artificiality of the privileged classes—they look at Nature through windows and have no feelings of their own. If we call it blank-verse journalism of a high order one imagines Auden would not object. A great deal of Louis MacNeice's work was of this kind, and Auden himself did write the verse commentary for a GPO documentary film.

But in the middle section of the poem Auden plunges beneath

the surface, with Sigmund Freud to help him identify the symptoms of the doomed society which Karl Marx has so clearly condemned. In other words, it seems that Auden has accepted the left-wing thesis that capitalist society is in decay ('The game is up,' Auden says to the financier, in the last section) and that he uses the Freudian notion of widespread neuroses as evidence of that decay. (The marriage of Freud and Marx is not unique to Auden: it was celebrated by several writers, notably Spender and Jack Lindsay.) Add to this Auden's memories of reading the doom-filled Anglo-Saxon and Scandinavian sagas, and his own relish for the sinister, observable in many poems, and we have the rather strange mixture of social comment and baleful warnings which Bayley identifies as 'schizophrenia' and Alvarez as 'hack-work'.

Some of this middle section is obscure because of the unexplained allusions: sometimes the syntax and punctuation are at fault. Bayley tells us that the 'supreme Antagonist' is the Freudian Death Wish which afflicts bourgeois civilisation and seemingly dooms the 'highborn mining-captains' as well as the 'handsome and diseased youngsters' and the female 'solitary agents in the country parishes'. There is something melodramatic about Auden's presentation of the sick members of capitalist society: one is hardly convinced of the danger or importance of 'ruined boys', brutal farmers or lonely women. So the mysterious rhetoric of doom-to-come also appears both vague and alarmist:

> Then, ready, start your rumour, soft
> But horrifying in its capacity to disgust
> Which, spreading magnified, shall come to be
> A polar peril, a prestigious alarm,
> Scattering the people, as torn-up paper
> Rags and utensils in a sudden gust,
> Seized with immeasurable neurotic dread.

35–41

There is a journalistic sensationalism about this vision of the Death Wish, scattering and seizing people, which is most manifest in the description 'A polar peril, a prestigious alarm'—this imitation *Beowulf* sounds too much like a burlesque of a newspaper headline. Freud's cool, prosaic essays on neurotic manifestations have been transformed into News from Nightmare City, by Our On-the-spot Reporter. Admittedly the Unconscious is a tough subject for poetry and Auden is not the only one who has struggled to find a suitable set of metaphors to express it. (Spenser, in *The Faery Queene*, I, i, had similar difficulties in describing the mechanism whereby a bad spirit from Hades supplied the Red Cross Knight's sleeping brain with sexy dreams.)

The third section makes more explicit reference to the capitalists and their allies. The financier will no longer need his typist and his boy, and the game is also up for those

> Who, thinking, pace in slippers on the lawns
> Of College Quad or Cathedral Close,
> Who are born nurses, who live in shorts,
> Sleeping with people and playing fives.

> 96–9

This rather extraordinary list of doomed types (for I presume it is not the dons and priests who wear shorts and sleep with people), together with 'Seekers after happiness', will all discover that 'It is later than you think'. This switch to rather slangy threats reminds one of C. Day-Lewis's jocular dismissal of the bourgeoisie, and seems rather inadequate in face of the 'polar peril' lurking explosively in the bourgeois unconscious. The final lines recall, not very relevantly, the atmosphere of a school prize-day, when

> Amid rustle of frocks and stamping feet
> They gave the prizes to the ruined boys.

> 54–5

(One asks: ruined already by the 'system', or sexually perverted, or what?) The middle-class escape from anxiety by means of motoring and its pleasures is rejected in two compact lines which exhibit Auden's talent for the memorable phrase:

> Not though you pack to leave within an hour,
> Escaping humming down arterial roads . . .

> 57–8

The final lines are enigmatic. It looks as though the fate of the bourgeoisie is to end in psychosis—either a 'mania' or a 'fatigue' —but there is no concluding clarity in these congested, obscure phrases:

> ... the prey to fugues,
> Irregular breathing and alternate ascendancies
> After some haunted migratory years
> To disintegrate on an instant in the explosion of mania
> Or lapse for ever into a classic fatigue.

59–63

This is the way the bourgeois ends, not with a bang but with a psychosis. However, the bourgeois has proved more resilient than the Thirties popularly supposed. Moreover, if the ruling classes are really as sick as Auden says, one wonders why in other poems he asserts that they can and should be cured.

This poem, handling as it does various notions from Marx and Freud, raises the question of whether Auden is merely a pedlar of fashionable ideas. Alvarez makes this accusation about the content of both Auden's verse and prose essays which, he says, 'is more a matter of quick and deft juggling with received ideas—from psychology, anthropology, sociology, and so on—than any real effort to get at something he knows, however obscurely, for himself'. Now it is true that some poets do give the impression of being intellectual magpies, alert for some glittering new idea with which to stun the reader, and today the temptation to reach for the up-to-date encyclopedia at the local library or the latest Penguin paperback on atomic physics must be hard to resist. (When Aldous Huxley travelled the world he took with him several volumes of the *Encyclopedia Britannica* for bedside reading: he, like H. G. Wells, was in the best sense a populariser of modern ideas and knowledge.) Some poets prefer to look into their hearts and write. Others write, or seem to write, only out of their own experience of the world. But one has only to recall Dante, Donne, Milton or Yeats, to realise that 'received ideas' from theology, science or esoteric philosophies are openly present in their verse. Indeed, it would be rather pointless for great theologians, scientists or philosophers to publish their ideas if poets were required studiously to avoid receiving and repeating them. Popularisation of this kind is surely a necessity in our society, and if poets, novelists and essayists do not fulfil this role then the pamphleteer and journalist will. That the poets of the Thirties read Marx and Freud is no more surprising than that the Victorians read Huxley and Darwin, or that the Augustans read Locke and Hobbes. All that we can demand is that the poet should digest the new ideas and incorporate them intelligently into his thinking and his poems. Of course one may consider Freudian and Marxist ideas to be half-baked anyway, and dislike Auden's poem for its ideological content, but my criticism is that, although I applaud Auden's attempt to make poetry out of ideas current in his period, I believe that his poetic treatment of them is bad. The poem is melodramatic, obscure, passing from one topic to another without any observable logic. Despite the promising opening section one is finally left disappointed.

When the Spanish Civil War began in 1936, with the attack by General Franco on the Republican Government, and the subsequent involvement of Hitler's Germany, Mussolini's Italy and Stalin's Soviet Union, as suppliers of armaments or troops, it seemed to left-wing supporters both a symbolic and a real struggle between the international forces of reactionary capitalism and progressive socialism. The International Brigade was formed and many English volunteers marched to join it, farewelled by Clement Attlee, his fist clenched in the Bolshevik salute. Writers such as Christopher Caudwell, Julian Bell and John Cornford were killed in Spain. Picasso supported the Government cause. The most celebrated poet and playwright of Spain, Federico Garcia Lorca, was murdered in mysterious circumstances —a murder laid at the door of the Fascists, though this has been disputed. Although in fact the Spanish War was a complex and confused struggle, it appeared to contemporaries as a clear-cut issue which could unite all anti-Fascists, and it caught the imagination of writers and evoked poems, novels and reportage infused with burning political passion. The last two issues of the magazine *Contemporary Poetry and Prose*, in 1937, carried the message

Arms for Spain on the back cover, and the editor left for Spain. In 1939 Stephen Spender and John Lehmann issued a collection entitled *Poems for Spain*, which included contributions by such writers as John Cornford, Richard Church, T. R. Wintringham, Stephen Spender, Herbert Read, Roy Fuller, Rex Warner, George Barker, Jack Lindsay, Edgell Rickword, C. Day-Lewis, Louis MacNeice, J. Bronowski, F. L. Lucas and W. H. Auden.

The poems in this volume range from satirical attacks on non-interventionists and descriptions of battle, to love poems and laments for bombed cities and murdered children. John Cornford ends a poem with the call:

> Raise the red flag triumphantly
> For Communism and for liberty.

Margot Heinemann's quiet and sensitive consideration of the war concludes: 'One nation cannot save the world for ever.' Tom Wintringham reports: 'Death means the girl's corpse warm-alive when buried.' Herbert Read laments 'Lorca was killed, singing', and Spender comments on an incidental casualty:

> The guns spell money's ultimate reason
> In letters of lead on the spring hill-side.
> But the boy lying dead under the olive trees
> Was too young and too silly
> To have been notable to their important eye.
> He was a better target for a kiss.

The Australian Jack Lindsay sees both the tragedy and the future hope:

> In the city-square the rags of bodies lie
> like refuse after death's careless fiesta.
> Sandbags are piled across
> the tramlines of routine.
> A bullet has gone through the townhall clock,
> the hands of official time are stopped.
> New clocks for the Spanish people:
> New springs and cogwheels for the Time of Freedom.

These brief extracts give some idea of the type of poems inspired by the Spanish War, but of course there must be scores of poems on this theme lying uncollected in the little magazines of the period. George Barker's long poem *Calamiterror* is an example of a major work devoted to Spain and related matters, and these few lines will indicate something of his mood and manner:

> The Welsh mountain weeps and the Cumberland fell weeps;
> London lies like a huge rot along the Thames, and Rome
> Roars. O Spain, my golden red, she tears the rot out,
> The Franco gangs that furrow in her heart. See how she stands,
> Her Madrid middle growing vague with ravage,
> Labouring to let out liberty, with the rat and the rot at her heart.

I think it is safe to say that the most famous poem on the Civil War was Auden's 'Spain'. It was published as a pamphlet in 1938 (the proceeds went to 'Medical Aid for Spain'), and reprinted in Spender and Lehmann's *Poems for Spain*. Three stanzas were deleted for the 1940 re-issue (in *Another Time*) and in this revised form it appeared in the *Collected Shorter Poems* of 1950. However, Auden only gave permission for it to be reprinted in its original form in the Penguin collection, *Poetry of the Thirties*, on the understanding that the editor, Robin Skelton, made it clear that Auden now regarded 'Spain' to be 'trash which he is ashamed to have written'. And the poem has been abolished from the new *Collected Shorter Poems, 1927–57*. In fact in the Foreword to this collection Auden writes:

> Again, and much more shamefully, I once wrote:
>
> > *History to the defeated*
> > *may say alas but cannot help nor pardon.*
>
> To say this is to equate goodness with success. It would have been bad enough if I had ever held this wicked doctrine, but that I should have stated it simply because it sounded to me rhetorically effective is quite inexcusable.

To Auden, as to many others, the Spanish issue posed a problem of moral choice. Auden has frequently distinguished between propaganda, which tells us what to do, and poetry, which presents a situation and invites us to decide on our attitudes and actions. As he put it in *The Poet's Tongue* (1935):

43

> Poetry is not concerned with telling people what to do, but with extending our knowledge of good and evil, perhaps making the necessity of action more urgent and its nature more clear, but only leading us to make a rational and moral choice.

Auden presented the choice before us by selecting a rhetorical structure which mirrored the situation as he saw it. This structure is a simple one, based on the three words: yesterday, tomorrow, today. The argument of the poem thus runs: *yesterday* man achieved certain things throughout his whole history on this earth; *tomorrow* there may be new opportunities for man; but *tomorrow* is not possible unless *today's* problem is solved. And today's problem is the political and military struggle in Spain, a struggle which will determine the future path of history. Of course, Auden assumes from the outset that the Spanish Civil War *is* a crucial struggle, fundamental to both Spanish and world future history, and he believes that one side in that struggle is right and the other is wrong.

It is true that he is not crudely the propagandist, telling us that we *must* take such and such action; his aim is surely to persuade us to act, and his persuasion takes the form of selecting various facts or arguments and binding them together with the repeated statement: 'But to-day the struggle.' What, we may ask, is the line between propaganda, or didactic exhortation, and urgent, rhetorical persuasion? It looks as though Auden has abandoned his usual 'clinical' assessment of a situation for a more traditionally polemical tone and persuasive rhetoric. The final lines, which Auden now finds to be 'wicked doctrine', state with overbearing insistence that history will not pardon us if we lose. As soon as a poet starts 'making the necessity of action more urgent' it is difficult for him not to appear partisan. (I don't personally see why a poet shouldn't be partisan, so long as he doesn't disguise his attitudes under the cloak of neutral objectivity.)

The opening section of six stanzas, at first sight without much logical coherence, rapidly sketches the history of man, primitive, medieval, modern, Eastern and Western. There are quick references to Chinese trade-routes, horse-taming, and railway-construction, which give a sort of shorthand guide to stages in economic evolution, but mixed with these are allusions to the development in human beliefs—the abolition of fairies and giants, the chapel in the forest, the carving of angels and gargoyles, trials of heretics, miraculous cures, witchcraft and lectures on the origin of mankind. The initial impression may be that Auden has simply ransacked an encyclopedia, but in fact the somewhat higgledy-piggledy list of human activities does remind us of the chaotic surface of human history, and has the same kind of puzzling but exhilarating attraction. For behind the chaos we always try to find a pattern, and behind Auden's historical snapshots there is the pattern of evolution—mainly scientific improvements and an accompanying development of religious beliefs from magic and witchcraft and heresy-trials to *lectures on evolution*. Such phrases as 'alarming gargoyles', or 'theological feuds', or 'the prayer to the sunset/And the adoration of madmen' seem to me to point to a fairly sceptical attitude to supernatural rites, and it is noteworthy that, in the corresponding list of possible human activities in the future, there is not a single reference to religious beliefs or ceremonies, unless the 'beautiful roar of the chorus under the dome' is that of a cathedral choir.

Auden's vision of mankind's past is certainly highly selective, but on the whole it is the sort of account which I imagine most up-to-date freethinkers of his generation would have found acceptable. It is not particularly Marxist: there is nothing about the class-struggle. (Marx had said that all the recorded history of mankind was the history of class-struggle.) Indeed there is not even much about *people*, except for the mention of unusual individuals such as navigators and heretics. The main emphasis is on inventions (cart-wheels or dynamos) or on religious manifestations. Is this, one asks, relevant to Spain, to the crucial 'struggle'? Perhaps the underlying implication is that Franco will uphold traditional Catholic Spain (gargoyles, heretic-trials and miraculous cures), and the features of modern civilisation (turbines, construction of railways, scientific lectures) will therefore not emerge or be adequately encouraged. The striking omission from this first section is any allusion to human freedom. The past seems to be mainly technological development and the discarding of superstitions. There is no concept of history as a process in which man slowly and arduously conquers greater areas of freedom—a concept which both Marxist and Whig historians might agree upon. It is true that in the final section Auden does mention the future as a time for 'fun under/Liberty's shadow', but if we look at the kind of things people will be able to do when they have Liberty—such as photographing ravens or holding bicycle races—one might wonder whether these activities are particularly threatened by a Franco victory.

In the second section (stanzas 7 to 14) three types of people are heard asking Life to help them. The nature poet demands 'the luck of the sailor'. The scientist, with microscope or telescope, says rather enigmatically: 'But the lives of my friends. I inquire. I inquire.' And the poor exclaim: 'Oh, show us/History the operator . . .' For some reason Auden finds the poet, the scientist, and the poor, representative of the nation: in fact 'the nations combine each cry' and address the Life Force which designed the evolutionary process. (Rather ingeniously Auden likens the levels of organisation of the sponge, shark, and robin, to a city state, a military empire and a canton.) The nations plead with the Life Force to intervene, to solve the problem which faces them, though the idea is couched in somewhat ironical terms—come, they say, as 'a dove or/A furious papa or a mild engineer'. The entire section in fact treats the cries for help with sarcasm rather than sympathy. (Perhaps the 'dove' is a call for divine intervention, and the 'furious papa' a comic coupling of the Victorian heavy father and the vengeful Jehovah of the Old Testament.) However, Life refuses to intervene: 'I am not the mover.' It declares (rather obscurely, I think) that Life, far from being a guide or a resolving force, is merely an abstract name for whatever a human being is. As Auden puts it, Life is the sum of all the separate items in one's life: it is the

> Yes-man, the bar-companion, the easily-duped;
> I am whatever you do. I am your vow to be
>   Good, your humorous story.
> I am your business voice. I am your marriage.

49–52

Life is therefore choice, and each individual must choose what his life, and life in general, is to be like. He can equally well 'build the just city' or make 'the suicide pact', and at this precise moment in history choice is symbolised by Spain, now for the first time mentioned by name in the poem: 'I am your choice, your decision. Yes, I am Spain.'

The existentialists do not of course have a monopoly in the notion of *choice*—the idea of free-will has been debated for centuries—but we are nowadays familiar with the prominent position *choice* has in the existentialist philosophy, and how in works of literature it generates tremendous emotional tension. We perhaps think of literary existentialism as a post-World War II movement, but it goes back to the early part of this century. Sartre was writing before the war, and André Gide popularised the idea of *l'acte gratuit* in *Les Caves du Vatican* (1914).

Stanzas 15 to 19 constitute a third section in which those who have chosen to aid Spain are described making their way to the war. Here the verse moves from simple, evocative detail to symbolism. First, there is the tone of unspectacular heroism:

> They clung like burrs to the long expresses that lurch
> Through the unjust lands, through the night, through the alpine tunnel;
> They floated over the oceans;
> They walked the passes. All presented their lives. — *what they'd made of their live.*
> 61-4

Then the thoughts and fears of the soldiers become identified with the Spanish landscape, so that the inner conflicts of men are transformed into the external conflicts of warfare: 'On that tableland scored by rivers,/Our thoughts have bodies; the menacing shapes of our fever/Are precise and alive.'

Auden's technique here is a type of symbolism, in which objects correspond to human attitudes or emotions, and verbally they are fused together. The process is not unlike the surrealist method of, for example, expressing unconscious ideas by means of images of limp watches hanging on a bough, or, to go back to the 17th century, the conceits of John Donne—in one of which, we remember, the love of a man and a woman was closely associated with the mechanism of a drawing-compass. Auden however, like the surrealists, adds a Freudian component to his symbolism. Somehow the 'fears which made us respond/To the medicine ad.' have been transformed into battalions (such as the International Brigade): our private neuroses, in other words, have become sublimated into aggressive intervention in the Civil War. (This peculiar psychological motivation seems decidedly less heroic than an early stanza had suggested.) On the other hand the brutal 'firing squad and the bomb' represent the concrete manifestation of human 'greed', and in our society this greed is symbolised in 'our faces, the institute-face, the chain-store, the ruin'. C. K. Stead in his article *Auden's 'Spain'*, in *London Magazine*, March 1968, identifies the battalions as Franco's, in which case the neuroses and the greed of modern society are shown as finding their outlet in Fascist aggression and brutality. Stead may be correct here, though it rather depends on whether 'invading battalions' refer to the anti-Franco volunteers, described as arriving from all quarters to fight in Spain, or to Franco forces, and whether 'our faces' refers only to Fascist tendencies within bourgeois society or to the faces of Franco invaders. Personally I think Auden sees the Civil War as a war within each individual bourgeois, and his Fascist tendencies are incarnated in Fascist activities and his good tendencies are embodied in good deeds. As the next few lines make clear, good tendencies within the human soul ('tenderness' and 'friendship') are now translated into medical rescue-work and service with the anti-Franco military forces:

> Madrid is the heart. Our moments of tenderness blossom
> As the ambulance and the sandbag;
> Our hours of friendship into a people's army.

74–6

Is Auden's technique successful? As we have seen, it is a rather complex method of psychological symbolism, whereby the inner conflict of Good and Evil in the soul is identified with the

48

conflict of anti-Fascist and Fascist on the Spanish battlefield. Technically it is rather startling. Franco's firing-squad is really a manifestation of Greed, and this in turn is manifested in our bourgeois society by the Chain-store (symbol of capitalist rapacity). The same sin lies behind both fascist brutality and capitalist 'private enterprise'. Again we note that Auden is marrying Marx and Freud, neatly equating bourgeois neurotic fear with aggression, and bourgeois greed with brutality. If you remove the specifically Marxist element you are left, however, with something not very different from a traditional Christian analysis: War is the result of Sin. The old-fashioned Christian used to say that War was God's punishment for man's Sin—indeed the Old Testament Jehovah frequently made this point to the Jews—whereas more modern Christians would, I think, prefer to call War a direct result of human Sin. It may seem surprising to find Freudian and Christian explanations of War to have similarities: 'War is the result of sinful greed and fear' is matched by 'War is the result of aggressive egotism and neurotic dread'. Many have suspected that Freud merely took the Christian notion of a struggle between God and the Devil for man's soul and, placing the struggle within the human unconscious, renamed the antagonists Super Ego and Id. Be that as it may, as far as Auden is concerned it is noteworthy that his Freudian-Marxist analysis of war, enclosed in surrealist symbols, is something which today, as a Christian, he may very well feel to be 'trash which he is ashamed to have written'. But his concepts are those of many men of the Thirties, faced as they were with that bewildering new force known as Fascism. And Auden's notion, in Marxist-Freudian terms, that Fascism was a moral disease latent in bourgeois society was clearly expressed in a quotation from Sir Peter Chalmers Mitchell, which was prefixed to the anti-Fascist collection *In Letters of Red*, 1938 (in which Auden's 'Dover' appeared):

> Fascism is a pathological condition, a disease of Society. Unfortunately it is contagious. Its leading symptoms are exaggerated selfishness and moral atrophy. In its more virulent phase, as in Germany, Italy and Spain, it glorifies and justifies crime. In its weaker forms,

as in the British Government and the majorities of the two Houses of Parliament, it appears as a complacent and selfish cowardice. But it is the same disease, and I fear that a very slight change in economic conditions would produce the virulent phase even in England.

Four stanzas only, 20 to 23, are devoted to 'To-morrow, perhaps the future'. As with the evocation of the past, the same technique of seemingly disparate snapshots is employed. The developments in science may continue:

> . . . the research on fatigue
> And the movement of packers; the gradual exploring of all the Octaves of radiation;
> To-morrow the enlarging of consciousness by diet and breathing.
>
> 77–80

As we noted earlier, there is nothing particularly socialist about the future, as one might have expected after a crucial victory over Fascism. (Perhaps time-and-motion study of packers seemed a progressive field of research at the time: trade unions have mainly rejected it as a boss's device for exploiting workers more efficiently.) At all events, most of the other items which Auden enumerates ('the rediscovery of romantic love', or 'the exchanging of tips on the breeding of terriers', or 'walks by the lake') seem to be chosen deliberately for their utterly non-political character. From the point of view of the central theme of a crucial 'struggle' which faces man with such an agonising choice, Auden's picture of the future, for which men are fighting and dying, might appear almost frivolous. (The only political activity mentioned is democratic voting, and that is suggested rather ironically as 'The eager election of chairmen/By the sudden forest of hands'.) It is possible to suppose that, in order to avoid the usual propagandist image of a brave new world of social justice, full employment, and proletarian culture, Auden purposely stressed a future where trivial pleasures or personal happiness ('the weeks of perfect communion') would once more be a matter of *choice*. In a sense this is a welcome touch, a refusal to wax polemical, an insistence on the value of life's everyday, intimate, even 'insignificant', activities. But I think this particular effect could have been made together with some indication that a future free of Fascism will have some additional qualities—for instance, freedom from Jew-baiting or the regimentation of youth. The logic of the poem surely demands that, if history has seen the replacement of 'alarming gargoyles' and 'the Sabbath of witches' by 'railways in the colonial desert' or 'the classic lecture', a similar process will continue in the future. One wonders, of course, how far Auden, for all his knowledgeable-ness about science, really felt excited about the scientific future. Somehow the past, 'the bustling world of the navigators', seems more interesting than the future, with its 'gradual exploring of all the/Octaves of radiation'. It may be that Auden's image of the future—a cold technological society escaping by means of 'romantic love' or simple 'bicycle races/Through the suburbs on summer evenings'—is a true mirror of reality, and that despite his 'clinical' pose he intuitively reacts against the scientific, socialist, planned society. My guesses may be wrong, but it is clear from the poem itself that Auden's vision of the future is not the optimistic, socially-orientated vision of the Marxist. He cannot say exultantly with the Soviet poet Mayakovsky's Loco Engineer (in *Mystery Bouffe*, 1918):

> We are the architects of earths,
> the planets' decorators;
> we are the wonder-makers.
> The sunbeams we shall tie
> in radiant brooms, and sweep
> the clouds from the sky
> with electricity.

One might ironically contrast the Auden of 1938, who can extol a future in which there will be 'the enlarging of consciousness by diet and breathing', with the sceptical Auden of 1944 who, recommending parents to read *Grimm's Tales* to their children, added: '. . . and then, in a few years, the Society for the Scientific Diet, the Association of Positivist Parents, the League for the Promotion of Worthwhile Leisure, the Cooperative Camp for Prudent Progressives and all other bores and scoundrels can go jump in the lake.'

The last three stanzas of 'Spain' return to the theme of 'But today the struggle'. Again this is presented by a catalogue of items, though rather less disparate, to suggest the quality of life imposed on us by war and political activity. It is not heroic or glamorous, but dangerous, monotonous and crude. War is accepted but as an inevitable evil: 'The conscious acceptance of guilt in the necessary murder,' and the routine of organising support for Spain is seen as a dismal 'expending of powers/On the flat ephemeral pamphlet and the boring meeting.' The personal life of the soldier is reduced to:

> To-day the makeshift consolations: the shared cigarette,
> The cards in the candlelit barn, and the scraping concert,
>   The masculine jokes; to-day the
> Fumbled and unsatisfactory embrace before hurting.

> 97–100

Modern warfare is grimly unpleasant and is only accepted with distaste. One sees how far the poets of the Thirties have travelled from some of the poets of the First World War, when we compare Rupert Brooke's words, written at Christmas 1914: 'But there's a ghastly sort of apathy over half the country and I really think large numbers of male people don't want to die—which is odd. I've been praying for a German air raid.'

Auden's final stanza expresses most openly the existentialist notion that man is an alien in a universe which is not conscious of his presence: 'The stars are dead. The animals will not look.' Neither the Life Force, nor the cosmos, nor Nature can help man, essentially alone as he is, to make his decision. The Nihilists, or our modern Absurdists, might retort—then why bother to act in a meaningless world? But Auden, like the existentialists, accepts man as the measure of all things, and it is man (under the abstract title, 'history') who will make the final judgment:

> We are left alone with our day, and the time is short, and History
>   to the defeated
> May say Alas but cannot help nor pardon.

> 102–4

Auden's 'Spain' is worth examining at some length for various reasons. It is a uniquely *public* poem, in which a specific political theme is presented for a presumably large and varied audience. The simple, though effective, rhetorical structure obviously is one way in which Auden managed to appeal directly to a mass audience, and, as C. K. Stead reminds us, when the poem is read aloud it reveals its compelling rhythms. (He adds: 'If one doubts the emotional authenticity of a poem one should listen to its music—and not all of those who have pronounced on Auden's poetry have been equipped with ears.')

But all too often the public, political poem adopts an earnest, strident, polemical tone which soon becomes monotonous or embarrassing. To take an American example—in *Proletarian Literature* we find Maxwell Bodenheim's lines 'To a Revolutionary Girl':

> ... you are a girl,
> A revolutionist, a worker
> Sworn to give the last, undaunted jerk
> Of your body and every atom
> Of your mind and heart
> To every other worker
> In the slow, hard fight
> That leads to barricade, to victory
> Against the ruling swine.

Admittedly Americans are less shy of rhetoric than are the reticent English, but in the Thirties the rousing call was also heard in England. Rex Warner's 'Hymn', 1933, is certainly triumphant, if not exactly churchy:

> There is no need now to bribe and to take the bribe.
> The king is flying, his regiments have melted like ice in Spring.
> Light has been let in. The fences are down. No broker is left alive.
> There is no pretence about the singing in the streets and the dancing.
> Come then, you who couldn't stick it,
> lovers of cricket, underpaid journalists,
> lovers of Nature, hikers, O touring cyclists,
> now you must be men and women, and there is a chance.
> Now you can join us, now all together sing All Power
> to lovers of life, to workers, to the hammer, the sickle, the blood.

> Come then, companions. This is the spring of blood,
> heart's hey-day, movement of masses, beginning of good.

(Presumably Mr. Warner was not singing this hymn in 1945 when he became Director of the British Institute in Athens.) Equally rhapsodic is the last stanza of Day-Lewis's *The Magnetic Mountain*, though, after all the sophisticated imagery of machinery and psychology, the poem ends with homely, rural evocations:

> Beckon O beacon, and O sun be soon!
> Hollo, bells, over a melting earth!
> Let man be many and his sons all sane,
> Fearless with fellows, handsome by the hearth.
> Break from your trance: start dancing now in town,
> And, fences down, the ploughing match with mate.
> This is your day: so turn, my comrades, turn
> Like infants' eyes like sunflowers to the light.

Auden's 'Spain' deliberately avoids this rather facile exuberance. His tone is urgent, but often prosaic ('the time is short'): profoundly serious, yet not baldly earnest ('the medicine ad. and the brochure of winter cruises'). The style varies considerably. There are abstract phrases, such as the 'private nocturnal terror'; slangy terms mixed with personifications, as in 'all the fun under/ Liberty's masterful shadow'; quick, suggestive combinations of an adjective and a noun—'the necessary murder', 'the shared cigarette', 'the masculine jokes'. But the dominant technical device is the heterogeneous catalogue, which enables him to range widely and rapidly over a topic (e.g. the history of mankind) and also to startle us with quick changes of tone or bizarre juxtapositions of phrases (the 'breeding of terriers' followed immediately by the 'eager election of chairmen'). Auden may have invented this device, or he may have noted something like it in Chaucer's *Prologue*, but the contemporary influence could have been the surrealist one. Surrealist poetry often employed sequences of seemingly unrelated images, usually startlingly absurd, and suggested (according to the theory of 'automatic writing') directly by the Unconscious, which has its own laws of image-association. Herbert Read composed poems according to this theory, but a more provocative practitioner of surrealist verse was David Gascoyne, who also, like Auden, wrote for *New Verse*. Here is a typical example of the catalogue-device from his poem 'And the Seventh Dream is the Dream of Isis' in the October 1933 issue of that magazine:

> 'white curtains of tortured destinies
> inheriting the calamities of the plagues of the desert
> encourage the waistlines of women to expand
> and the eyes of men to enlarge like pocket-cameras
> teach children to sin at the age of five
> to cut out the eyes of their sisters with nail-scissors
> to run into the streets and offer themselves to unfrocked priests
> teach insects to invade the deathbeds of rich spinsters
> and to engrave the foreheads of their footmen with purple signs
> for the year is open the year is complete
> the year is full of unforeseen happenings
> and the time of earthquakes is at hand'

Of course Auden's catalogues, as we have seen, do have an underlying theme, but they have the same kind of surface effect of disparate, incongruous images, and Auden also has something of the surrealists' liking for the humour of surprise effects—the deliberate banality of 'the assessment of insurance by cards' or the unusual juxtaposition in 'theological feuds in the taverns'. But unlike the surrealists he binds together his varied items with overt conscious logic instead of the nightmare logic of the Unconscious.

And so 'Spain' remains in many ways a symbol of the Auden of the Thirties, revealing his technical experimentation of the time (polemical rhetoric, surrealist catalogues, etc.) and his Freudian-Marxist-Existentialist vision at a moment when a critical political problem demanded from him some kind of poetic manifesto. This manifesto he has now repudiated, a sure indication of a fundamental change in outlook which we shall study when we deal with his more recent work.

3

Pop Poems

Perhaps each age has its own form of light verse and to Auden, as well as to such writers as John Betjeman, E. E. Cummings, T. S. Eliot or Ogden Nash, we must be grateful that our own century has realised the importance of not being earnest. It may be true that light verse does not travel well, either from country to country or from generation to generation. The arch, over-emphatic joking of the Victorians is now no more to our taste than the endless verbal juggling in some of Shakespeare's comedies, though if we read Partridge's *Shakespeare's Bawdy* we can glimpse a layer of sexual innuendo which the Elizabethans must have appreciated. It remains to be seen whether Auden's varied experiments in light verse will prove more durable, but at least these poems have a ready appeal for contemporary readers, and in this sense one could apply the modish term 'pop poet' to Auden.

In his collected essays Auden has given us thoughtful and amusing 'Notes on the Comic', which indicates his serious interest in the comic. He has edited the *Oxford Book of Light Verse* and expressed his admiration for writers such as Edward Lear, Ronald Firbank, P. G. Wodehouse and John Betjeman. The surrealistic humour in *Paid on Both Sides*, and in the plays written in collaboration with Christopher Isherwood, perhaps is derived from continental example—the general influence of Dadaism and Surrealism and the particular influence of Brecht. In the essay 'Translating Opera Libretti' Auden has some fascinating pages on the problems of turning Brechtian humour into good American, and he gives this as an example:

Now she shows off her white little fanny,
Worth twice a little Texas motel,
And for nothing the poolroom can stare at Annie
As though she'd nothing to sell.

The 'schoolboy humour' of the prose sections of *The Orators*, the sustained pastiche of Lord Byron in *Letters from Iceland*, and many passages of parody in *The Age of Anxiety*, testify to Auden's attraction to the comic mode, and recent poems such as 'Goodbye to the Mezzogiorno' or 'On Installing an American Kitchen in Lower Austria', later called 'Grub First, then Ethics (Brecht)', show that he is still inventing new forms of light, but not frivolous, verse.

Because light verse can also be serious it is valid to make a study of this important aspect of Auden's output. I have also the hunch that light verse often betrays the author's social and personal attitudes more revealingly than so-called serious verse. When Eliot unbends in his comic volume for children, *Old Possum's Book of Practical Cats* (1939), his affection for a certain middle-class world and its values is manifest. A good deal of Auden's latest verse (much of which might be classified as light) deals with either the academic environment or his private life among friends, who are frequently fellow-artists or belong to the cultured middle-classes. (In 'The Common Life' in his 1966 volume *About the House*, he says: 'the homes I warm to,/though seldom wealthy, always convey a feeling/of bills being promptly settled/with checks that don't bounce.') But these personal poems are mainly quite recent. The earlier light verse springs from experiments with popular forms or styles, such as ballads, blues, or jazz-lyrics, which are public and objective, by and large, though one can no doubt deduce from them Auden's own attitudes.

We can only roughly put Auden's light verse into groups: inevitably there is some overlapping. Five convenient labels might be: Social Comment, Highbrow Pop, Jazz, Blues and Ballads, and I shall look at a selection of his work under these headings. It is noticeable that quite a large number of these poems appeared between about 1935 and 1945, and the fact that many were printed in periodicals and collections such as *New Writing, The Listener, New Verse, New Statesman* (and one was written as a documentary film commentary) indicates probably that Auden was looking for and finding a wider audience than before. This attempt to speak to people not normally accustomed to reading fairly difficult poetry, may have encouraged him to see whether such popular styles as found in jazz-lyrics or blues songs could be used to express his ideas or comments. In a similar way the plays written with Isherwood were means to reach a greater public, though I think it is clear that they never had more than a minority appeal. Naturally, those who consider that Auden's interest in Marxism and left-wing revolution merely led him to a middle-class flirtation with proletarian movements, to 'boyscout Communism', will probably feel that his blues and ballads are nothing more than intellectual slumming or, at best, a slick attempt to exploit a fashionable idiom-of-the-masses. We have certainly seen enough of the commercial abuse of Negro jazz or genuine folksong, and the degradation of language by the sensationalist press, and we are rightly suspicious of Ethnic Folksong born in glossy recording studios. Even beatnik verse and anti-establishment musicals have been known to reap a golden profit for entrepreneurs who know how to turn protests against society into the latest daring vogue. (One remembers that Shaw's early protests against his society were feared and banned. When he became accepted by the middle-class theatre-goers as their licensed buffoon his social criticism was dismissed as the crankiness of a witty, Irish rogue.) Those who suspect Auden merely of dabbling with more popular poetic forms could easily show that he is not a genuine Negro inheritor of the jazz and blues tradition, nor a street-ballad singer, and that he is more familiar with the campus, the lecture-theatre and the library than with the arduous life of peasants or factory-workers. (J. M. Cohen, in *Poetry of this Age*, attacks Auden sharply for his 'fundamental poverty of experience' and questions 'whether he takes the creative process at all seriously' in his 'off-hand ballads'.) But this is exactly the problem of the bourgeois poet today. His experience of life *is* usually limited. If he is to speak to readers outside his own class he must seek new themes and styles. When the middle-class, university graduate, William Wordsworth, started to write about peasants in simple English he was ridiculed by his educated, urban contemporaries. Of course, Wordsworth wasn't a shepherd or a leech-gatherer and inevitably, despite his imaginative sympathy, he viewed the rural working-class from outside—hence his tendency to idealise them, and the absence of detailed description of their work. But until shepherds and leech-gatherers begin to write their own poetry (and I believe they will) it will be composed for them by interested poets, visiting sociologists or, at worst, paid hacks of the tourist industry. (The crude American travelogue—'And so we say farewell to Coconut Island, etc.'—is the commercialised attempt to poetise another culture.) Wordsworth's lyrical ballads have their limitations, but were they not an advance on the make-believe pastorals of the 18th-century gentlemen for whom peasant life was merely an excuse for fantasy pieces in an idyllic never-never land? We can therefore, I think, welcome Auden's attempt to experiment with popular verse-forms, just as we welcome Ezra Pound's efforts to make Provençal or Chinese poetry available to us. We shall remain aware of the risks of 'intellectual slumming' or modish exploitation of novelty, but the real test is whether Auden's poems succeed as poems.

SOCIAL COMMENT

The first group we might examine shows Auden using a rather flat, colloquial style to make social comments. The language is deliberately 'unpoetic', on the whole, and the tone varies between deadpan irony and simply-expressed awareness. 'Musée des Beaux Arts', published in Spring 1939, is a reflection upon the unspectacular way in which human suffering occurs in, as it were, a corner of the picture, while the rest of life continues oblivious of it. Auden mirrors the effect of life, disinterestedly and trivially pursuing its random course, in the trailing line: 'While someone else is eating or opening a window or just walking dully along.' He says that the Old Masters painted the 'miraculous birth' or the 'dreadful martyrdom' fully aware that nearby 'the torturer's horse/Scratches its innocent behind on a tree'. In the second half of the poem Auden describes Brueghel's *Icarus* (in which the large, solid peasant ploughman fills most of the picture, and a tiny figure in the distance is the falling Icarus). One critic has interpreted this painting as Brueghel's manifesto of Northern Realism's superiority to Classical Mythologising, but Auden's point is that ordinary life—ploughing, the sailing ship on the sunlit sea into which Icarus is falling to his death— ignores the 'disaster', the 'important failure', the 'something amazing'.

One might say that Auden's philosophical comment about Life is not itself startlingly original or profound, and the relaxed, conversational tone ('Where the dogs go on with their doggy life') casual to the point of being *blasé*, as though the observer is merely a tired journalist doing a routine job. But this effect is deliberate, and calculated to shock. Life is teaching us not to be romantic about suffering, death, martyrdom or disaster. They are part of the landscape, and the landscape doesn't care or know about them. The sensitive poet faces the outer world, which seems to ignore his existence; important human events, significant to each individual, are lost in the anonymous routine of social living, of nature— these may well have been the thoughts which lie behind this poem. That Auden is *not* a bored journalist but involved in the clash between meaningful action and the alien surrounding world, is seen in his use of adjectives which put a value on certain events: 'miraculous birth', 'dreadful martyrdom', 'important failure'. Behind the controlled verbal surface we feel the anguish of one who has registered the fact of human suffering, taking place in isolation from an unseeing, uncaring environment. The poem balances between moral revulsion, because 'everything turns away/Quite leisurely from the disaster', and acceptance of the nature of things. In the last images we see quite simply that though there are individual disasters, life must continue:

> . . . and the expensive delicate ship that must have seen
> Something amazing, a boy falling out of the sky,
> Had somewhere to get to and sailed calmly on.

19–21

No doubt interpretations will differ. Some may find this ending too detached, or too brutal. I would call it sensitive acceptance. There is neither petulant protest at human suffering, nor swaggering stoicism. There is both 'the forsaken cry' and the ship sailing 'calmly on'. Certainly it mirrors the superficial 'philosophy' of the newspaper reader who calmly notes the devastating earthquake in Peru as he spreads a little more butter on his breakfast toast, but it points also in the direction of a religious acceptance of suffering. That one should link the two experiences is not surprising, for any adequate religious outlook today must base itself on the chaotic world revealed to us through the daily newspaper: this is the 'absurd' world with which religion must come to terms.

'Who's Who', published in 1936 in *Look, Stranger!*, alludes indeed not to newspapers but to that famous publication which lists the outer manifestations of fame. (The entry under *Auden* is a good example of how a man's life is reckoned in terms of academic decorations, medals and prizes.) The rhymed sonnet form, assessing a man within fourteen strict lines, is an appropriate way of imitating the *Who's Who* catalogue of external items. Indeed Auden parodies the slick itemising of a life when he says that the cheap biography (the 'shilling life') will relate how 'he fought, fished, hunted, worked all night,/Though giddy, climbed new mountains; named a sea....' That this mechanical thing, composed of mere activities, should beneath his social mask be actually human is emphasised by the debunking colloquial language:

> Some of the last researchers even write
> Love made him weep his pints like you and me.

(The slangy phrase, 'weep his pints', is not a concession to popular taste, but a deliberate device to reduce the mythical celebrity to normality.)

Auden's frequent awareness of the clashing public and private aspects of life is clearly shown in the contrast between the 'greatest figure of his day' and the one who lived insignificantly and trivially at home, pottering about the garden and whistling. (If we take 'sighed for' to mean 'was in love with', rather than 'envied', then this 'one' must be a woman, to whom he writes long, marvellous letters. But it is possible to interpret it to mean a different type of man whose life he envied.) The nonentity is deliberately made to seem socially useless, untalented, uncreative. It would be nice to think the poem poses the age-old theme of the Active versus the Contemplative Life—but there is not much evidence that she does much contemplating, even though she does 'sit still'. Nor is the poem simply an assertion that the stop-at-home-and-do-nothing kind of existence reflects some sort of holy virtue. It seems to me that Auden is saying that both public and private lives can, in their different ways, be empty. The form of the poem makes one expect that, after the deflating of the celebrity, the contrasting figure will be the poet's ideal. John Holloway (in his article 'The Master as Joker') claims for her a 'private integrity' because she 'did little jobs about the house with skill', and no doubt Auden intends this admiringly, but what private integrity can be implied by her whistling, sitting still, pottering round the garden, or answering letters? Unless Auden has suddenly become sentimental this is a picture of private integrity operative at a trivial level. The empty grandiosity of public life is paralleled by the harmless banality of private life. As a 'pop poem' it makes its social comments by simple language and catalogue-devices, and its diagnosis of the modern division of human existence into either a public life of frantic activity, or a private life of pleasant inactivity, has a challenging clarity.

From the shilling life of a famous man we may turn to the satirical portrait of the average man, or, as Auden entitles him, 'The Unknown Citizen' (which was first published in *The Listener* in August 1939). The colloquial language and the every-day allusions to frigidaires, radios, instalment plans, trade unions, etc., make one immediately at home with this poem, and a few lines will allow us to sample its type of irony:

> Our researchers into Public Opinion are content
> That he held the proper opinions for the time of the year;
> When there was peace, he was for peace; when there was war, he
> went.

He was married and added five children to the population,
Which our Eugenist says was the right number for a parent of his
generation . . .

The poem is a compilation of details about the average man, written in the flat, matter-of-fact tone of a report. His work at Fudge Motors factory, his union membership, the newspaper he bought, etc., etc., are all listed in the manner of the social survey questionnaire, and the various bureaucratic spies (the Bureau of Statistics, Producers Research, High-Grade Living) are all satisfied that he is average and normal. Only at the very end does the question arise: 'Was he free? Was he happy?', and the answer given is: 'Had anything been wrong, we should certainly have heard.'

This poem, light though it appears, is attacking the concept of a human being who is not much more than the product of all the economic, commercial and ideological pressure-groups which force him to conform to a standard pattern of life and thought. Modern mass-organisations, such as the factory or the trade union (and even peace and war can be considered in this way), impose a uniformity on the individual, and this is strengthened by the press and the educational system. Any personal variations are immediately spotted by Social Psychology workers, or other bureaucratic corrective mechanisms, and commerce of course is an interested party for it sells the average citizen his 'necessary' phonograph, radio, car and frigidaire. In his academic satire, 'Under Which Lyre', Auden is in 1947 to assert that the individual must not kowtow to administrative or intellectual conformism. Here, in 1939, on the eve of war, Auden protests against a society which manipulates man by the laws of mass-organisation, commercial exploitation and a social research spy system. This kind of criticism of the extinguishing of individual freedom and happiness came, and still comes, from men of very different viewpoints. The novels of D. H. Lawrence exposed the effect of modern society on man's emotional life. Left-wing thinkers attacked not mass-organisation of society itself, but the capitalist exploitation of that society (and in his Thirties poems

Auden voiced similar views). But of course the hatred of all forms of bureaucratic controls and mass conformism can be found in a wide range of people, in anarchists and in liberals, in aristocrats who disdain mass-society or in Christians who fear its effect on spiritual freedom. Auden's particular standpoint is hard to establish. He seems as hostile to commercialism as to social surveys. Perhaps the divergence from a left-wing analysis is most obvious in his picture of the factory and the trade union:

> Except for the War till the day he retired
> He worked in a factory and never got fired,
> But satisfied his employers, Fudge Motors Inc.
> Yet he wasn't a scab or odd in his views,
> For his Union reports that he paid his dues,
> (Our report on his Union shows it was sound) ...

6–11

This makes a neat bit of irony but can we accept the implication that for men in the post-1918 period it was possible to be a satisfactory worker (and not fired during the Depression) and at the same time a satisfactory Trade Unionist? There may be times when Capital and Labour have collaborated happily, but hardly in the Twenties and Thirties. How did an Unknown Citizen manage to avoid the repercussions of the General Strike of 1926 or the economic crises of the Thirties—when three and three quarter millions in Britain were unemployed by 1932? In his attempt to show how the average person is pressed into conformism by *all* social forces, Auden has had to ignore that within modern society there are often deep conflicts *between* these social forces. Apart from the obvious conflicts of Labour and Capital, there are the population problems (where 'High-Grade Living' and 'our Eugenist' may set very different targets) and the supply-and-demand problem in a society in which 'advertisements' and 'Producers Research' demand free spending, whereas the boom-slump economy produces unemployment and periods of austerity. These, and other, profound conflicts, which are equally characteristic of modern mass-society as are the conformist influences, make the average citizen a prey to dangerous forces which Auden should not have ignored. His picture of the socially-regimented citizen is false because he lives in a materialistic Utopia where he is fully employed, 'fully insured', in perfect health, and provided with all the luxury items available. (Were cars normal for the average man in this period?) Auden is projecting his fears about a middle-class Utopia on to the factory-worker's existence, which cannot be as docilely and prosperously conformist as Auden imagines. Of course, the poem can still serve as a warning against the social pressures of our mass-society, but Auden's diagnosis is too superficial. He identifies the conformist influences but seems unaware of the huge conflicts generated by modern society. If he had forgotten the General Strike and the Slump he must today, in America, be witnessing the ugly tensions of a system which has unsuccessfully tried to impose modern types of conformism upon its Unknown Citizens.

'Night Mail', written in 1935 as a commentary for a GPO film, shows that Auden could supply the simple type of descriptive verse required by a documentary film. No doubt film-verse, like film-music, is not intended to be separated from the film of which it originally formed an integral part, but Auden's lines can stand on their own. Perhaps we cannot blame him for discovering nothing terribly profound or exciting in the modern postal system, in which the drama is limited to the humdrum vision of 'the Night Mail crossing the Border,/Bringing the cheque and the postal order . . .'. As one might have expected, the commentary mainly tries to capture the visual details of the train 'Shovelling white steam over her shoulder' or 'Snorting noisily', while the birds turn and stare at the 'blank-faced coaches'. We are not far from the happy world of the children's picture-book, with its coy presentation of machines as animals, and its primary-colour illustrations. In one or two verses Auden neatly mirrors the film's ability to communicate by means of a telling detail:

In the farm she passes no one wakes,
But a jug in a bedroom gently shakes.

15–16

Auden's talent for catalogue-effects is seen in the description of the letters:

> The chatty, the catty, the boring, the adoring,
> The cold and official and the heart's outpouring,
> Clever, stupid, short and long,
> The typed and the printed and the spelt all wrong.
>
> 40–3

The postal service may be an essential part of an economic system, but it is on a personal note that the poem ends:

> And none will hear the postman's knock
> Without a quickening of the heart.
> For who can bear to feel himself forgotten?   51–3

Perhaps one shouldn't pause too long over a poem of this kind, though one notes that Auden has found a place for it in his *Collected Shorter Poems* of 1966. I don't know how far Auden had to comply with directions from the film-producer, but it looks as though documentary film-verse must remain very simple in its effects. However, one cannot judge by a single example. A satirical film, or a lyrical cinematic exploration of country scenes, for example, might stimulate a very different type of verbal sound-track. All we can say is that Auden has now turned his attention to a more traditional form of artistic co-operation— the composition of opera libretti.

Auden's colloquial poems of social comment do not figure very conspicuously in his total work, especially if we compare his output with the stream of volumes published by another Birmingham-domiciled friend, Louis MacNeice, whose fluent pen reflected the middle-class urban world of the Thirties and Forties with satire-tinted faithfulness. (One thinks of his poem, 'Birmingham', and his vision of suburbia:

> In these houses men as in a dream pursue the Platonic Forms
> With wireless and cairn terriers and gadgets approximating to the
>   fickle norms
> And endeavour to find God and score one over the neighbour
> By climbing tentatively upward on jerry-built beauty and sweated
>   labour.)

One suspects that Auden has not got the journalistic eye which swoops so rapaciously on the myriad details of social life, and exhibits them in lengthy, descriptive poems. And one wonders whether Auden has sufficient intimate experience of the varied aspects of modern life. From the provincial school staff-room the view is a little limited, and one cannot expect Auden to give us an authentic evocation of working-class life, as Sean O'Casey did in his plays or Richard Hoggart in *The Uses of Literacy*, nor a profound sociological document on our civilisation, as a trained sociologist might do. Presumably Auden responded to his times and attempted to develop a popular social-comment verse, but there is not a great deal, and only very occasionally does he explore this vein in his more recent work. One of the rare examples is 'Fleet Visit', published in *The Shield of Achilles*, 1955, among poems which display a mock-heroic debunking of many features of our civilisation. In the poem entitled 'The Shield of Achilles' some of the stanzas refer grimly to contemporary cruelties:

> Barbed wire enclosed an arbitrary spot
>> Where bored officials lounged (one cracked a joke)
> And sentries sweated for the day was hot:
>> A crowd of ordinary decent folk
>> Watched from without and neither moved nor spoke
> As three pale figures were led forth and bound
> To three posts driven upright in the ground.

In 'Fleet Visit' the style is more jauntily colloquial—in fact, rather disarmingly like a popular song:

> The sailors come ashore
> Out of their hollow ships,
> Mild-looking middle class boys
> Who read the comic strips . . .

The details of the 'natives', the whores they encounter, and the military reasons for the visit, are mentioned rather casually. It could easily be the report of a friendly journalist. But the last two stanzas undeceive us, though the critical comment is made with great artistic reticence. The ships 'on the dazzling blue' seem innocent because 'Without a human will/To tell them whom to kill/Their structures are humane'. But this machine beauty, which makes them seem mere functionless works of art, is revealed as an illusion—for no government is going to spend enormous sums of money on a useless aesthetic construction. Auden makes the point quietly, simply by ending with a vulgar appraisal of their worth in terms of hard cash. One would not praise anything humanly valuable by referring to its market value; the ships, however,

> Look as if they were meant
> To be pure abstract design
> By some master of pattern and line,
> Certainly worth every cent
> Of the millions they must have cost.

Is the irony perhaps too quiet? The public critic (one thinks of Dryden or Pope) usually makes his satirical points pretty obviously, just in case the less sensitive reader should miss them. Of course, one can be subtle and sophisticated, but the irony must be recognised. (There have been notorious cases of ironical poems being taken seriously.) Auden's use of a mixture of popular song and newspaper story idioms perhaps does not prepare us for the critical ending, which relies on the contempt generated by the smell of dollars in the last two lines. At all events one must contrast this delicate effect with the more emphatic Drydenian satire of 'The Truest Poetry is the most Feigning' (in the same group of poems), in which Auden addresses a love poet and describes how, when occasion demands, the poet can easily transform his ode to his mistress into a flattering eulogy of the new political leader:

> If half-way through such praises of your dear,
> Riot and shooting fill the streets with fear,
> And overnight as in some terror dream
> Poets are suspect with the New Regime,
> Stick at your desk and hold your panic in,
> What you are writing may still save your skin:

Re-sex the pronouns, add a few details,
And, lo, a panegyric ode which hails
(How is the Censor, bless his heart, to know?)
The new pot-bellied Generalissimo.
Some epithets, of course, like *lily-breasted*
Need modifying to, say, *lion-chested*.
A title *Goddess of wry-necks and wrens*
To *Great Reticulator of the fens*,
But in an hour your poem qualifies
For a State pension or His annual prize,
And you will die in bed (which He will not:
That silly sausage will be hanged or shot).

47–64

The traditional heroic couplet has trained us to respond to certain satirical devices. Auden's use of the popular lyric, and reticent ironical effects, is another example of his inventive skill, and no doubt readers will become sensitive to this low-keyed mode of satire, which I find refreshingly sly and gentle. One wonders whether the Dryden-Pope mock-heroic tradition can be successfully revived today. Roy Campbell's *The Georgiad*, in 1931, had plenty of gusto. Indeed as Guy Butler, a fellow South African poet, once put it, it has all the characteristics of Pope—except the subtlety. Auden has achieved satirical subtlety within, surprisingly enough, a much more popular form than the urbane heroic couplet.

JAZZ POEMS

The second group of popular poems which we may look at seems to be influenced by jazz lyrics. The term *jazz* is a rather vague one, including perhaps the original Negro music in America, various commercialised imitations of it, and national types of this cosmopolitan style such as that found in Brecht and the German cabaret song (which Auden would have been familiar with during his stay in Germany). It is clear that many poets and composers were attracted to the jazz idiom—one may mention in passing the *Threepenny Opera* score by Kurt Weill, the 'symphonic jazz' experiments of Walton and others, or the play,

Sweeney Agonistes, by T. S. Eliot (which has successfully been produced recently to an accompaniment of bongo drums). C. Day-Lewis, Louis MacNeice and many American poets wrote an imitation or parody of jazz lyrics, and one scene in Ronald Duncan's *This Way to the Tomb* uses jazz idiom to satirise a new entertainment-type religious service. One of the ironies of such jazz-religion pieces, which were intended to shock readers in the earlier years of this century, is that they are now much less daring than the pop-religion services which have become almost commonplace. In 1969 go-go dancers were performing in the crypt of St. Paul's Cathedral; at St. Jude's, Southsea, the Rev. David Churchman delivers sermons through a ventriloquist's dummy; dancing groups have been introduced into Presbyterian Churches during services; the guitar and Beatle-type groups often replace the organ and choir. Even the Oxford University Press has issued a new-look Old Testament, with illustrations of naked girls or of 'a modern-day business executive, wearing horn-rimmed glasses, contemplating a half-naked woman in black tights'. The Archbishop of Canterbury is reported as saying of this edition: 'The result is really rather exciting, a service to religion and art.' In other words jazz-culture, and similar experiments, have now invaded traditional or 'highbrow' spheres to such an extent that the novelty of Auden's jazz-poems has been considerably reduced.

In the 1933 edition of *Poems* (1928) Auden replaced item IX by one which begins:

> It's no use raising a shout.
> No, Honey, you can cut that right out.
> I don't want any more hugs;
> Make me some fresh tea, fetch me some rugs.
> Here am I, here are you:
> But what does it mean? What are we going to do?

Later Auden discarded this poem, but it has been popular with anthologists. Though the general meaning is apparent—the bewildered speaker rejects the facile 'love' offered in popular songs, and expresses his disillusionment and state of inactivity—

the specific significance of some of the images is hard to deter-mine. Does the leaving of the mother represent an unresolved Oedipus complex (as Monroe Spears suggests) and is there an allusion to the Theory of Evolution in the lines: 'In my veins there is a wish,/And a memory of fish'? As with most of Auden's jazz-poems it is not easy to say whether the flat, colloquial style and novel imagery are an imitation or a parody of jazz-idiom. If we associate jazz-lyrics with facile sentiments and superficial ideas, then it is hard to take seriously what Auden writes in this idiom:

> In my spine there was a base;
> And I knew the general's face:
> But they've severed all the wires,
> And I can't tell what the general desires.
> Here am I, here are you:
> But what does it mean? What are we going to do?

But the main flaw in the poem is its vagueness. We don't know who the speaker is, what type of person he represents, why he can find 'No land, no water, and no love', why and how 'life fails', or why he lies 'crying on the floor'. The mood of baffled depression is conveyed successfully but we'd like to know a little more about the man (or woman?) and the situation. We are not sure whether we are asked to criticise or sympathise. Admittedly jazz-lyrics often are mere mood-pieces, but usually the cause of the mood is mentioned, or is too obvious to mention. (Moods without any apparent cause form the basis of many of Bob Dylan's powerful but vague compositions.)

'Danse Macabre' is a puzzling 'popular' poem for different reasons. It was first published in *The Listener* in February 1937, and two stanzas were omitted in the 1965 collection. In the 1966 collection the first two lines: 'It's farewell to the drawing-room's civilised cry,/The professor's sensible whereto and why,' have been changed to: 'It's farewell to the drawing-room's mannerly cry,/The professor's logical whereto and why'. This meticulous revision would suggest that Auden has not retained an old poem without careful scrutiny of it, yet Beach in his lengthy comments on this short poem (in *The Making of the Auden Canon*, pp. 191–202) remains bewildered that Auden can still subscribe to 'a work intended for the consumption of liberals in the know' when he is now 'a Christian poet in 1945'. Another problem that Beach raises is that Auden allowed part of this pacifist, anti-capitalist, pro-Devil poem to be set to music by Benjamin Britten in 1939 to honour men who had fallen in the International Brigade in Spain.

Leaving aside these contextual complications we turn to the poem itself, which proves to be an attractively bouncing song in which Auden has married the rushing rhythms of the old street-ballad with sophisticated modern vocabulary and allegory. The old-fashioned world of courtesy and logic is farewelled, together with

> The frock-coated diplomat's polished aplomb,
> Now matters are settled with gas and with bomb.

Culture (the 'works for two pianos' and other 'frangible wares') is stored upstairs, for this delicate civilisation is threatened by none other than Satan:

> For the Devil has broken parole and arisen,
> He has dynamited his way out of prison,
> Out of the well where his Papa throws
> The rebel angel, the outcast rose.

9–12

The speaker identifies himself as the 'Fortunate One' whose destiny it is to chase the Devil and 'rid the earth of the human race'. He equates human society with Sodom and Gomorrah, and declares he must employ liquid fire to 'storm the cities of human desire'. From these and further details we gain the impression that, as in other Thirties poems, Auden is adopting the tactics of attacking an enemy by allowing him to speak and reveal himself. But who exactly is he? Seemingly the old blend of puritan and capitalist who is to rid the earth of human desire, 'irreverent thinking', not to mention 'eating and drinking'. To accomplish this he will recruit 'Little John, Long John, Peter and Paul' to wage a suicidal war against the Devil:

A scene from the first performance of *The Dog Beneath the Skin* by the Group Theatre at the Westminster, London, 1936

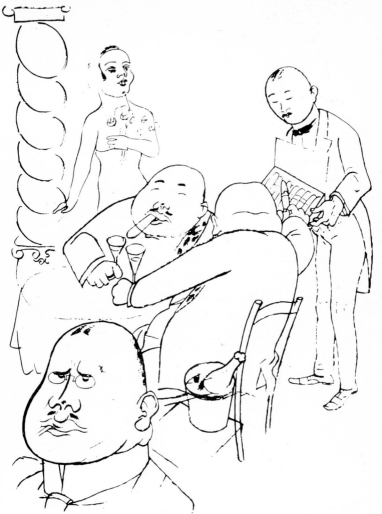

'Esplanade' by George Grosz (1893–1959). This drawing comes from *Ecce Homo*, a collection which bitterly attacked pre-war German society

> For it's order and trumpet and anger and drum
> And power and glory command you to come;
> The graves will fly open to let you all in,
> And the earth be emptied of mortal sin.

49–52

The Enemy's puritanism and militarism are manifest, but the identification with capitalism is less obvious, although we note that he does himself greedily appropriate all the benefits of the material world:

> I shall have caviar thick on my bread,
> I shall build myself a cathedral for home
> With a vacuum cleaner in every room.

38–40

Bourgeois fine food, religious architecture and modern gadgets are in fact enjoyed by the capitalist class which primly exhorts the workers to stop sinning and lusting after the flesh. Here, as in other poems, Auden hits at bourgeois hypocrisy and its use of Christianity as a class-weapon. We are not surprised that in the process bourgeois culture (the pictures and piano pieces are stored upstairs) will become as vulgar and exhibitionist as a motorcade or street carnival:

> I shall ride the parade in a platinum car,
> My features will shine, my name will be Star,
> Day-long and night-long the bells I shall peal,
> And down the long street I shall turn the cartwheel.

41–4

Even if we can assemble this jigsaw-puzzle of an Enemy, he remains something of an eclectic jumble of fairy-tale 'spoilt Third Son', military leader, woodchopper's axe, caviar-eating motorcade star (cartwheeling in his spare moments) and, in the last stanza, a crooner ('So good-bye to the house with its wall-paper red'). Add to this his rabid puritanism and the picture becomes complicated. The allegorical speaker is nearer to the grotesque masked figures in expressionist drama, or to the start-ling effects of a surrealist painting, than to the simpler allegorical characters we are used to in Spenser's *Fairie Queene* or in medieval plays. In attempting to integrate many features of decadent capitalism into his Enemy persona, Auden has forsaken the clarity which one expects in a poem written in a popular idiom. But even more confusing is the equation of the progressive forces with the Devil. Logically enough the puritanical speaker, at home in his cathedral, sees his foe as the Devil, as Sodom and Gomorrah, as 'human desire', as 'mortal sin'. To eradicate these from the face of the earth really requires a war that will annihilate humanity. The tactics of the poem demand that the speaker pictures his foe as a rebel angel, walking abroad 'like influenza' (one remembers the fearful epidemics of the period), and dragging his 'dear' to 'depths of shame'. These phrases reflect the neurotic bourgeois fear of the liberating forces of Freud and Marx (expressed frequently by Auden in these years) but it is difficult to sympathise with progressive forces presented exclusively by their Enemy and in terms of traditional Christian abhorrence. To reverse one's usual reactions and remember that 'influenza', 'adders', 'unsound' trees, and Sodom and Gomorrah, are really the Enemy's terms for wholesome, revolutionary, sexually-fulfilling forces of progress, or that 'mortal sin' is really sane Freudian freedom, is too much to expect of the reader. William Blake attempted this particular kind of irony when he equated God with all the negative and aggressive forces of society and the Devil with the principle of liberty. Startling though the initial impact may be, it is difficult to sustain this topsy-turvy device because all other words denoting good and evil must be changed too. In Auden's poem, for example, one may be able to register inwardly that the Enemy's term 'Devil' symbolises for us 'Good', but when the Enemy tries to frighten the reader by saying that the Devil walks abroad 'like influenza' we have to suppress our normal revulsion at epidemic diseases and register the topsy-turvy equivalent—whatever that may be. And so it continues until all the vocabulary of the poem is affected. Therefore, despite the poem's rhythmic vitality and originality of phrase, its would-be popular appeal is strangled by its excessive complexity. There seems little point in using the attractive jazzy ballad idiom, with its simple clarity of language, if one is

74

going to import into the poem a mystifying polemical structure of allegory and verbal topsy-turvydom.

As I have said, it is only possible to place Auden's popular poems into rough categories. 'As I walked out one Evening', for instance, has the strophic form and other features of the ballad, and Auden himself has referred to it as a 'pastiche of folksong'. Yet the type of imagery used reminds us so much of the brash yet somehow piquant awareness of the jazz-lyric idiom that we might well consider it here. It was published in January 1938 in the *New Statesman* and is still in print in the 1966 collection. Elizabeth Lutyens provided a musical setting for it between 1954 and 1956. As in the earlier poem 'It's no use raising a shout' there is a rejection of popular ideas of love, and this is presented in the first five stanzas by the imitation of a banal song by a lover under 'an arch of the railway'—a pointed modern stage-direction. Here the extravagant and facile images of the commercial 'syrup number' are parodied:

> 'I'll love you till the ocean
>   Is folded and hung up to dry
> And the seven stars go squawking
>   Like geese about the sky.'

13–16

This trite sentimentality is answered by the clocks with their traditional warning 'You cannot conquer Time'. Reality is both more sinister and more petty, for although it destroys nature, culture and individual achievements (valley, dance and diving), it often works through commonplace maladies or anxiety:

> 'In headaches and in worry
>   Vaguely life leaks away,
> And Time will have his fancy
>   To-morrow or to-day.
>
> 'Into many a green valley
>   Drifts the appalling snow;
> Time breaks the threaded dances
>   And the diver's brilliant bow.'

29–36

Within life's activities, either splendid or banal, Auden sees the hidden hand of Time, and therefore in one sense the eternal is always present in the temporal. This leads to a stanza, in the same jazz-idiom as the lover's song, in which everyday objects are linked to symbols of menace. As though in a nightmare vision one can glimpse the emptiness behind life's homely details:

> 'The glacier knocks in the cupboard,
>   The desert sighs in the bed,
> And the crack in the tea-cup opens
>   A lane to the land of the dead.'

Time thus forces us to see through the actual world of cupboards, beds and tea-cups (and all they symbolise) to the reality, which is not the sentimental dream of the lover's song, nor the fictitious land of fairy tales. In the 'land of the dead', that is, the *real* world we live in, sometimes 'the Giant is enchanting to Jack' and innocent nursery-rhyme Jill 'goes down on her back'. But although Time reveals the 'distress' of man, whose 'tears scald and start' when he confronts reality, there is still the assurance that 'Life remains a blessing' and imperfect man is commanded to love, imperfectly, his imperfect fellow-man:

> 'You shall love your crooked neighbour
>   With your crooked heart.'

55–6

The moral is a Christian one and the tone both realistic and optimistic. 'It's no use raising a shout' had ended with a series of bewildered questions: 'But what does it mean? What are we going to do?' This later poem provides some of the answers. Technically it is less ambitious than 'Danse Macabre', but one must also add that it is more successful. The jazz-idiom has been used for an evaluation of the world which has proved to be *not* sentimental, as the lover's song proclaimed, but yet just as amazing as his extravagant metaphors suggested. For it *is* amazing that this tawdry world of cracked tea-cups, seduced Jills and crooked hearts, should 'remain a blessing'. Fallen man and his fallen world are worthwhile.

A few years later, in 1944, Auden employed popular idiom here and there in an explicitly Christian poem, *For the Time Being*, described as a Christmas oratorio, mainly to stress the topical relevance of the biblical story. We need not pause over this work except to display a sample of it taken from the section dealing with the temptation of St. Joseph. When Joseph speaks we are immediately brought forward to our modern world:

> My shoes were shined, my pants were cleaned and pressed,
> And I was hurrying to meet
>   My own true Love . . .

1–3

The temptation takes place in a bar and a scandalmongering chorus off-stage asks:

> Joseph, you have heard
> What Mary says occurred;
> Yes, it may be so.
> Is it likely? No.

10–13

Here the contemporary setting and colloquial idiom are a simple means of modernising history—a device which has become fairly commonplace and which can be seen in such works as Anouilh's *Antigone*, Sartre's *Les Mouches*, Guy Butler's *Judith*, Eliot's 'Journey of the Magi', W. R. Rodgers' 'Lent', Ferlinghetti's 'Christ climbed down', to mention but a few.

A more recent example of jazz idiom appears in the volume *Nones* (1951). 'The Love Feast', a phrase which has a specific Christian meaning, is described in terms of a modern drunken party. Gathered in an upper room at midnight and listening to the radio-phonograph the 'congregation' indulges in gossip and sexy adoration:

> Louis telling Anne what Molly
> Said to Mark behind her back;
> Jack likes Jill who worships George
> Who has the hots for Jack . . .

5–8

The Christian love feast and the degenerate modern parody of it are suggested by the vocabulary. 'Catechumens' (converts under instruction before baptism) enter and

> Steep enthusiastic eyes
> Flicker after tits and baskets;
> Someone vomits; someone cries.

10—12

Various types of love are evoked in neat, colloquial lines. Here it seems that the popular idiom is being used to stress vulgarity, sensuality, lack of sensitivity—to repel us, not to attract us. The final stanza juxtaposes the trite clichés of modern sex life with a famous remark by St. Augustine (in the last line):

> But that Miss Number in the corner
> Playing hard to get . . .
> I am sorry I'm not sorry . . .
> Make me chaste, Lord, but not yet.

25—8

Perhaps this last line is made by the speaker, whose identity in any case is not very clear. Presumably the Augustinian sentiments are not the moral of the poem, but an ironical comment on modern sexual hypocrisy. At all events it is noteworthy that jazz-idiom and traditional religious terms ('love according to the gospel', 'worship', 'sinner', etc.) are used to make a simple but telling contrast between Christian ideals and actual behaviour with regard to love. In other poems the jazz-idiom has been employed to satirise sentimental love, or puritanical capitalism, or St. Joseph's tempting scandalmongers, and here it is used to suggest sexual vulgarity. It looks as though Auden in general regards the jazz-idiom as a debased form of expression, suitable indeed to invoke debased attitudes found in contemporary society. An interesting comparison could be made with certain American Beat poets who have adopted jazz-idiom as a sympathetic medium for communicating their view of life, and as a valid popular language to set against the correct English of the Establishment. (See for example Ferlinghetti's moving poem on Christ's crucifixion, 'Sometime during Eternity', which speaks in this kind of language: 'Him just hang there/on His Tree/ looking real Petered out/and real cool/and also . . . real dead.')

Three poems which Auden labels 'blues', and one calypso, show similarities with the poems we have just studied. The song later named 'Funeral Blues' was originally a shorter piece in *The Ascent of F6* (1937), where it functioned as a burlesque lament for a secular saviour. As it now appears in the 1966 collection, without a title again, it should be regarded simply as a parody of a blues, with the characteristic flat language, dragging rhythms and exaggerated imagery. One stanza guys the triteness of the blues idiom:

> He was my North, my South, my East and West,
> My working week and my Sunday rest,
> My moon, my midnight, my talk, my song;
> I thought that love would last for ever: I was wrong.

9–12

This sort of parody, and the brash images ('Pack up the moon and dismantle the sun') are amusing in themselves and seem, in general, to belong to Auden's criticism of sentimental moods and overstated emotions. 'Refugee Blues', published in *New Writing* in Autumn 1939, takes, on the other hand, a serious, topical subject and treats it in an unexpected manner. Here Auden accepts the blues idiom as worthy enough to express important human sentiments:

> Saw a poodle in a jacket fastened with a pin,
> Saw a door opened and a cat let in:
> But they weren't German Jews, my dear, but they weren't German Jews.

Most of the poem catalogues the plight of refugees ('If you've got no passport you're officially dead') and suggests the inhumanity of officialdom as well as the selfishness of citizens, safe and secure in their 'mansions'. The contrasting freedom of fishes and birds is alluded to and politicians are specifically mentioned as though they were the main enemy of freedom:

Walked through the wood, saw the birds in the trees;
They had no politicians and sang at their ease:
They weren't the human race, my dear, they weren't the human
race.

Although there is no element of burlesque in this poem, we
feel perhaps a lingering uneasiness at the literate manner imposed by the subject-matter upon a form which is so strongly
associated with relatively illiterate Negro laments, with their
characteristic problems and emotional expressiveness. This
experiment by Auden raises the question whether certain cultural
modes, intimately connected with specific groups and their
milieux, can be transplanted to different social groups. On the
other hand, by casting the German refugees' lament in the blues
form, Auden has made us bring together in our minds the
sufferings of both Jews and Negroes at the hands of our society.

The three-line blues stanza is not followed in 'Roman Blues'
(published in *Another Time*, 1940) and though the language is
mainly flat and colloquial there is a laconic brevity about the
style which differentiates it from the usual repetitive manner of
genuine blues:

Over the heather the wet wind blows,
I've lice in my tunic and a cold in my nose.

The poem seems to me a wholly successful reminder of the banal
stupidities of war, everywhere and at all times. The soldier doesn't
know what he is doing, his grouses are the usual ones ('I want
my girl and I want my pay') and his comment on Christianity
is the sort of caricature of the truth that we are all guilty of
when we speak of somebody else's beliefs:

Piso's a Christian, he worships a fish;
There'd be no kissing if he had his wish.

Also in the same volume appeared 'Calypso' (dropped in 1945
but reprinted in 1966) which in idiom seems to me nearer to
Negro blues than to West Indian calypso, and in any case the
locale is 'Grand Central Station, New York'. Here there seems
no particular reason for using a West Indian form, a Negro

idiom and a New York situation for a love song which verges on parody:

> He presses my hand and he says he loves me,
> Which I find an admirable peculiarity.

We are not surprised at the contrast between the poor but happy lover and the banker, for popular song ideology always denies that the rich can be really in love:

> But the poor fat old banker in the sun-parlour car
> Has no one to love him except his cigar.

And this leads Auden to finish the song with an assertion which he frequently makes elsewhere, although here we feel the affirmation of love's significance isn't based on much more than trite sentimentality:

> For love's more important and powerful than
> Even a priest or a politician.

This poem illustrates well the problem Auden faces in putting serious ideas in the guise of popular song. Unfortunately the folk lyric (especially in its commercialised form) is only too ready to purvey pleasant, home-spun philosophies—in particular on the topic of love—and it is now hardly possible for a genuine poet to imitate it without being tainted by its facile sentimentality. So although Auden's experiments are to be applauded, one should expect some failures.

BALLADS

Perhaps the largest group of these experiments are the ballads, ranging from the old, traditional folk-poems to the racy street-ballads and the moralising Victorian types. An early example is 'O What is that Sound', previously called 'Ballad' or 'The Quarry', which originally appeared in *New Verse* for December 1934. Like the traditional ballads this poem presents a dramatic situation, without comments, by means of question-and-answer dialogue between a woman and a man who forsakes her—a standard situation of the old folk ballads. The language and the references to soldier, doctor and farmer, seem carefully chosen to be practically timeless. We sense the folk-ballad origin but there are no period-piece archaisms and quaintness as we find in 19th-century pastiche. (Spears suggests that in 1934 the nightmare image of soldiers brutally intruding upon private citizens was an appropriate parable of the inadequacy of romantic love as an escape from public events.) The pattern of the dialogue is of rapid questions by the woman (in the hurried anapaestic beat and ending with a word repeated as though in horrified unbelief), answered by the man in briefer lines, laconically and deceptively unemotional:

> O what is that sound which so thrills the ear
>> Down in the valley drumming, drumming?
> Only the scarlet soldiers, dear,
>> The soldiers coming.

1—4

The tension increases as the soldiers approach, their weapons glinting, wheeling past the doctor's, the parson's and the farmer's home, to run finally up to her locked door, which they violently smash. The last two stanzas form a powerful and terrifying climax:

> O where are you going? Stay with me here!
>> Were the vows you swore deceiving, deceiving?
> No, I promised to love you, dear,
>> But I must be leaving.

> O it's broken the lock and splintered the door,
>> O it's the gate where they're turning, turning;
> Their boots are heavy on the floor
>> And their eyes are burning.

29—36

We do not in fact want any more circumstantial details about the situation. It is a poem which presents us with the quintessence of betrayal and violence as simply and as timelessly as a medieval ballad. It is an amazing achievement.

Two comic-horrific songs which have upset some critics are 'Miss Gee', set to the tune of 'St. James' Infirmary', and 'Victor', set to 'Frankie and Johnny'. These were both published in *New*

Writing, Autumn 1937, and have suffered some revisions over the years. Despite the blues tunes to which they are written, the popular form they resemble most is the Victorian music-hall song (both the comic and the moralising varieties), and it is interesting to find humorous and sentimental anecdotage has once more found favour in songs for pop-groups—some of the Beatles' numbers are of this type. If the 'cruelty' of Auden's ballads reminds us of the 'sick jokes' of our current period, we should also remember the callous humour of Belloc's *Cautionary Tales*.

'Miss Gee' is the story of a poor, plain and puritanical maiden lady whose repression of sexual impulses leads to her developing cancer. Auden's belief that physical illness could be caused by sexual repression is openly voiced by the doctor:

> 'Childless women get it,
>   And men when they retire;
> It's as if there had to be some outlet
>   For their failed creative fire.'

73–6

When read (aloud for preference) the deliberately trite language and the slapstick humour are simply very funny. She dreams, for instance, that as she is speeding along on her cycle a bull, with the face of her vicar, is charging at her with lowered horn:

> She could feel his hot breath behind her,
>   He was going to overtake;
> And the bicycle went slower and slower
>   Because of that back-pedal brake.

33–6

Hilarious stanzas like this one, and the macabre comedy of the dissection of Miss Gee's corpse, set us an aesthetic problem because we are invited by the humour to participate in the mockery, to laugh at genteel poverty on 'one hundred pounds a year', at her squinting left eye and lack of bust, at her Church Bazaar knitting and her shocked avoidance of 'loving couples'. Of course, Auden could have presented Miss Gee as a pathetic figure and demanded our sympathy. Instead he has taught us a sharper lesson. We laugh (as we all do) at repressed old maids and then, as the anecdote proceeds gaily to its grim conclusion, we are made to feel not merely sorry but ashamed. The cruelty we find in the poem is our own cruelty, and Auden's expression of it is therapeutic, not sadistic. This is not the only way in which an artist may present human suffering, but it is an honest way, for it recognises the element of cruelty in our social behaviour. Miss Gee is afraid of normal love, but normal lovers also are too selfish to care:

> She passed by the loving couples
> And they didn't ask her to stay.

43–4

Readers have often questioned the relevance of the final stanza. What, says Joseph Warren Beach, would Oxford Groupers be doing in a London operating room? The answer is—something quite irrelevant, dissecting *her knee*. Trust the Oxford Groupers (another term for believers in Moral Rearmament), says Auden, to be looking for the cause of Miss Gee's sexual repressions in her knee.

'Victor' is a comic Victorian melodrama written in the form of a ballad. It is the tale of a 'mousey' bank cashier whose goody-goody piety is the result of paternal puritanical indoctrination. Not, perhaps, that a regard for 'the family name', telling the truth, or remaining pure in heart, can as such be labelled puritanism, but Auden's comic details suggest that Victor's religious instruction was purely theoretical, having no contact with concrete living:

> Victor and his father went riding
> Out in a little dog-cart;
> His father took a Bible from his pocket and read,
> 'Blessed are the pure in heart.'

9–12

The naïve and untested piety of Victor, reading his Bible in bed at the 'respectable boarding-house', is hardly of any help to him when he falls madly in love with the seductive Anna, who, for no very convincing reason, finally agrees to marry him.

84

When Victor accidentally hears the other clerks boasting of their affairs with Anna ('God, what fun I had with her/In that Baby Austin car') he weeps, and in bewilderment questions the God he had been taught to believe in:

> Victor looked up at the sunset
>   As he stood there all alone;
> Cried; 'Are you in Heaven, Father?'
>   But the sky said 'Address not known.'   85–8

In his tormented state he hears voices telling him to kill Anna, and there follows the Chaplinesque mixture of comedy and horror as Victor chases Anna round the house with a carving-knife:

> She dodged behind the sofa,
>   She tore down a curtain rod,
> But Victor came slowly after her:
>   Said, 'Prepare to meet thy God.'

129–132

(In the original 1937 version there is an additional stanza of farcical pursuit but this was later dropped.) After he has murdered Anna like an avenging religious fanatic, Victor is taken away in a van, insanely calling himself 'the Son of Man':

> Victor sat in a corner
>   Making a woman of clay:
> Saying; 'I am Alpha and Omega, I shall come
>   To judge the earth one day.'

145–8

Originally there was the refrain, 'Have mercy, Lord, save our souls from Hell,' between stanzas. This may have stressed the religious irony of the poem but no doubt it was a rather obvious effect and it interrupted the flow of the narrative unduly. As in 'Miss Gee' there is a sharp attack on the main figure by means of crude music-hall humour, and in addition there is the melodramatic farce of the pursuit. This may be an irreverent way to criticise a narrow and unworldly type of religiosity, but then Auden is trying to shock us out of conventional attitudes. If Victor were merely the butt of a comic anecdote we might feel the poem was frivolous, but the final stanzas engage our sympathy for Victor, who is a victim, not a clown. A Christian education which does not prepare Victor for an encounter with women like Anna is a mockery of religion, and there is splendidly bitter irony in the lines in which the redeeming blood of Christ is only Victor's demented distortion of what is really the blood of the wife he has slain:

> He stood there above the body,
>   He stood there holding the knife;
> And the blood ran down the stairs and sang,
>   'I'm the Resurrection and the Life.'   137–40

'Johnny' (now untitled, and beginning 'O the valley in the summer where I and my John') was one of the 'Cabaret Songs for Miss Hedli Anderson' and was published in 1940 in *Another Time*. It is a fairly simple parody of a popular love song in which the trite vocabulary mirrors the sentimental naïvety of the girl, who obsessively continues to adore the unresponsive man:

> 'Squeeze me tighter, dear Johnny, let's dance till it's day':
> But he frowned like thunder and he went away.   5–6

The courtship rituals of the day—the 'Charity Matinée Ball' and the 'Grand Opera' identify the girl as middle-class—are seen through the ecstatic eyes of the girl, though we smile when she says Johnny is as 'slender and tall as the great Eiffel Tower' and the comic rhythm always reminds us that the love affair is rather ridiculous:

> While the flowers at our feet and the birds up above
> Argued so sweetly on reciprocal love . . .   3–4

But the old ballad theme of the betrayed woman calls for a sombre ending, and within the banal idiom of the song Auden manages a note of shared pathos:

> O last night I dreamed of you, Johnny, my lover,
> You'd the sun on one arm and the moon on the other,
> The sea it was blue and the grass it was green,
> Every star rattled a round tambourine;
> Ten thousand miles deep in a pit there I lay:
> But you frowned like thunder and you went away.   25–30

This kind of poem—is it a parody or an imitation?—raises the question of whether the *simple* language of the traditional ballads can be replaced by the *debased* language of the commercial cabaret song. If we can appreciate the unsophisticated lament of a medieval maiden why should we snobbishly sneer at the modern equivalent? Is 'The floor was so smooth and the band was so loud' lesser poetry than this medieval 'definition of love' in ballad idiom:

> Love is soft and love is sweet, and speaks in accents fair;
> Love is mighty agony, and love is mighty care;
> Love is utmost ecstacy and love is keen to dare;
> Love is wretched misery; to live with, it's despair.

Was the medieval maiden any less sentimental than our contemporary swoony teenager, or her disloyal lover less crude than frowning Johnny? At all events, Auden's modern ballads challenge us to scrutinise our standards of judgment.

And so to the jolly drinking song. Two examples of Auden's more rollicking vein are 'Master and Boatswain' and 'Song of the old Soldier', both published in *For the Time Being*, 1944. The first one appears in the prose and verse commentary on Shakespeare's *The Tempest*, called *The Sea and the Mirror*, but we may discount its contextual significance and treat it as a separate sea-shanty, for Auden reprinted it simply as a song in his self-selected volume (Penguin, 1958). Its comic gusto appeals immediately:

> At Dirty Dick's and Sloppy Joe's
>   We drank our liquor straight,
> Some went upstairs with Margery,
>   And some, alas, with Kate . . .

A deeper meaning and untraditional imagery are found however in the concluding stanza:

> The nightingales are sobbing in
>   The orchards of our mothers,
> And hearts that we broke long ago
>   Have long been breaking others;

Tears are round, the sea is deep:
Roll them overboard and sleep.

This admixture of surrealist sophistication transforms the sea-shanty into something else—I'm not quite sure what, perhaps 'Song for the S.S. Salvador Dalí'. This modernistic treatment is more apparent in the second example, which formed part of the section 'The Massacre of the Innocents' in the Christmas Oratorio entitled *For the Time Being*. First there is a provocative interior monologue by King Herod: 'Why should He dislike me so? I've worked like a slave. Ask anyone you like. I read all official dispatches without stopping. I've taken elocution lessons. I've hardly ever taken bribes. How dare He allow me to decide? I've tried to be good. I brush my teeth every night. I haven't had sex for a month. I object. I'm a liberal. I want everyone to be happy. I wish I had never been born.' Then follows the song of the soldiers, 'When the Sex War ended with the slaughter of the Grand-mothers. . . .' Here the popular army-song form is used as the vehicle for intellectual slapstick along surrealist lines:

> When the Vice Crusades were over he was hired by some
>   Muscovites
> Prospecting for deodorants among the Eskimos;
> He was caught by a common cold and condemned to the whiskey
>   mines,
> But schemozzled back to the Army.
> *George, you old Emperor,*
> *How did you get in the Army?*

Here, I think, we see Auden's experiments with popular ballad being pushed into forms of satire too esoteric to appeal to a wide audience. It is strange to contrast this 'intellectual ballad' style with the deliberately traditional 'Lauds'. This is printed in *The Shield of Achilles*, 1955, but in a slightly different version formed the final chorus of the opera *Delia*, 1953, and it has been set to music by Lennox Berkeley. The form of 'Lauds' is the medieval Spanish *cossante*, couplets with an unchanging refrain and a complicated pattern of repeated lines, giving the effect of a dance-like, uncoiling movement, slow and dignified. Despite the complex organisation the result is of controlled simplicity. The poem stresses the sanity and joy of 'this green world temporal' and the communal spirit—the 'mass-bell goes dong-ding', God is asked to 'bless the People', and 'Men of their neighbours become sensible'. In cold print the medieval lyrical freshness has a somewhat faded look. No doubt the musical setting is required to support the rather thin verbal texture of stanzas such as this:

> The dripping mill-wheel is again turning;
> Among the leaves the small birds sing:
> *In solitude, for company.*   19—21

LATER POEMS

This in fact brings us to the later Auden, who still offers us experiments in popular modes, though the models are seldom if ever jazz or blues. One might even call these later examples 'highbrow pop' in that although the styles will have popular appeal the subject-matter is rather restricted. 'T the Great' (in *Homage to Clio*, 1960), for example, has lines as simple as doggerel (faces 'That wore expressions of alas on them,/And plains without a blade of grass on them'). But unless we solve the crossword anagram in the final stanza ('11 Down—A NUBILE TRAM') we won't realise that the poem is really a complicated historical comment on Tamburlaine the Great. 'A Toast', printed in *About the House*, 1966, is a more recognisable, comic-nostalgic 'Varsity poem, written for the 1960 Christ Church Gaudy, and thus a 'public' poem but written for a select few. Less astringent than a piece by Auden's admired John Betjeman, its obvious jocular rhythms and conventional facetiousness make it uncomfortably like a sentimental after-dinner speaker on a duty visit:

> Ah! those Twenties before I was twenty,
> When the news never gave one the glooms,
> When the chef had minions in plenty,
> And we could have lunch in our rooms.

> In *Peck* there were marvellous parties
>> With bubbly and brandy and grouse,
> And the aesthetes fought with the hearties:
>> It was fun, then, to be at *The House*.   9–16

Auden was at Christ Church from 1925 to 1928, writing poems about 'Life stripped to girders, monochrome. Deceit of instinct...'. In the Twenties there was civil war in Ireland, disorder and communal riots in India, guerrilla bands in Egypt, and in Britain the General Strike of 1926. And yet Auden can pleasantly recall it as a time when 'the news never gave one the glooms'. The convivial Gaudy atmosphere has resulted in indulgent reminiscences in the stuffiest Establishment idiom. Sometimes Auden is too good at pastiche. What is the point of a poet of original talent imitating a donnish poetaster?

Also in *About the House* is another of Auden's fairly rare personal poems, in which he gently debunks himself in his role of visiting celebrity, descending from the clouds to lecture briefly to a group of assembled citizens, only to be whisked away the next morning:

> Though warm my welcome everywhere
> I shift so frequently, so fast,
> I cannot now say where I was
> The evening before last...   ON THE CIRCUIT 17–20

The form and the language put this poem into our 'popular' class, and perhaps nowadays the highbrow entertainer is sufficiently common to be the subject of general appeal. The whole modern business of organised culture-for-the-masses is humorously guyed by the theological terminology:

> An airborne instrument I sit,
> Predestined nightly to fulfil
> Columbia-Giesen-Management's
> Unfathomable will,
>
> By whose election justified,
> I bring my gospel of the Muse
> To fundamentalists, to nuns,
> To Gentiles and to Jews...   5–12

The social commentary found in earlier popular verse is now only indirectly conveyed through the Poetic Evangelist's rather grumpy reaction to the modern scene. A 'sulky fifty-six', he dislikes a 'luxury hotel' and cannot 'bear with equanimity/The radio in students' cars,/Musak at breakfast, or—dear God!—/Girl-organists in bars'. He reveals also that his most anxious thought is always *What will there be to drink?* and wonders whether he dare take a swig from the bottle in his bag. The modern evangelist, we see, is a somewhat grubby version of our imagined biblical spreaders of the good news—though no doubt St. Paul had the Ephesian equivalent of girl-organists to contend with. In so far as the flying lecturer is a significant feature of our cultural landscape this poem is more than a self-critical personal portrait, and it closes on the note of ironic acceptance of the writer's contemporary role in American society:

> God bless the lot of them, although
> I don't remember which was which:
> God bless the U.S.A., so large,
> So friendly, and so rich.

61–4

Perhaps the 'gospel of the Muse' can remain untainted by commercial sponsorship, although one still wonders whether St. Paul would have consented to operate under the Columbia-Giesen-Management. It is a matter of how far a poet can come to terms with the means of extending his audience, and in the varying experiments with popular forms and idioms Auden has throughout his life been tackling this problem. It may primarily have been for him experiments with technique, but inevitably this meant adopting, rejecting or criticising attitudes and viewpoints which the popular idioms incorporated. Writing a folk-ballad, a blues, or a Gaudy poem involves the author in the cultural worlds of which they are a part. At the worst, Auden is a chameleon who blends perfectly with the chosen form and idiom. At his best he makes an established convention do something excitingly new.

4

Manifestos Public and Private

Auden confesses to a passion for detective stories, and to some extent we are required to play the detective when we study a series of his poems in which the poet, either in a private or public way, takes stock of the situation, reflects upon it, and sometimes expresses hopes or fears for the future. I refer to this group for convenience as 'manifestos', without wishing to imply that they are polemical banners unfurled dramatically to a massed audience. Our talents as detectives are needed, partly because the poems often include topical or personal allusions, and partly because Auden has chopped and changed some of them during the course of years. (A detailed examination of these alterations is given in Beach's *The Making of the Auden Canon*.) It would be an exaggeration to claim that in these poems Auden is striving to play the role of public prophet or adviser to the national conscience, in the manner of Dryden during the turbulent 17th century, but we do gain the impression that he is thinking aloud on various problems which have both personal and public aspects. The poems I shall deal with in detail are not the only ones of this type, but they do appear specially significant as well as being interesting as poetry. A chronological approach would seem sensible and it is probable that the poems were composed only shortly before publication, often in periodicals.

'1929'
Several of these works do include the date in the title, as though Auden was conscious of pausing at a specific time to consider himself and his period. The poem '1929' (originally number xvi in *Poems*, 1930) begins on a personal note:

> It was Easter as I walked in the public gardens
> Hearing the frogs exhaling from the pond,
> Watching traffic of magnificent cloud
> Moving without anxiety on open sky—
> Season when lovers and writers find
> An altering speech for altering things . . .   1–6

Beneath the unanxious sky the young man of twenty-one or so feels that change is in the air, and his sense of urgency is perhaps increased by the suffering around him—the solitary man, weeping on a bench, his distorted mouth 'Helpless and ugly as an embryo chicken'. This leads to his recalling personal friends and enemies, the 'once hated master' or his 'friend Kurt Groote'—at which point we may guess that Auden is in Germany, spending a year there after leaving Oxford. Yeats, perhaps, had started the modern vogue for bringing one's friends into one's poems: they have to be rather significant people if the effect of cosy, private cliquishness is to be avoided.

The second section introduces us to a feature of Auden's early style to which John Bayley has attached the very adhesive label 'pidgin English'. Auden wished to make his language more compressed, perhaps after the example of the Anglo-Saxon he had studied at Oxford, and so he began to delete pronouns, articles and other particles which are so frequent in English. But the clipped, urgent effect usually seems artificial, and the sense obscure:

> Coming out of me living is always thinking,
> Thinking changing and changing living,
> Am feeling as it was seeing . . .
>
>   34–6

Frequently Auden compares the life of man with that of surrounding nature. Here he opposes a passage about ducks who 'Sit, preen and doze on buttresses' against an evocation of the political turmoil in Germany, where for once the jerky style catches the panic and ugliness of the incidents like a rapid news-reel shot:

> All this time was anxiety at night,
> Shooting and barricade in street.

> Walking home late I listened to a friend
> Talking excitedly of final war
> Of proletariat against police—
> That one shot girl of nineteen through the knees
> They threw that one down concrete stair—
> Till I was angry, said I was pleased.

45–52

This violence is contrasted with the older way of life: 'From village square voices in hymn . . .' Contemplating this, as a 'Tiny observer of enormous world' (and how often in his poetry does Auden adopt this stance of observing from a distance), he then muses on such things as growth from infancy to manhood, man's solitariness, forgiveness, love. The style is rather obscure, despite a few telling phrases, such as 'Perfunctorily affectionate in hired room'. Various psychological writers, such as John Layard, Homer Lane, Freud and Groddeck, and authors such as Gide and D. H. Lawrence, had made speculations about man's psychic development popular, but Auden's thoughts about the child's passage from the womb to the world are phrased very awkwardly, like notes jotted from a text-book:

> Is first baby, warm in mother,
> Before born and is still mother,
> Time passes and now is other,
> Is knowledge in him now of other,
> Cries in cold air, himself no friend.

62–6

All that we can gather from this section is that within man there are also destructive forces—the Death Wish—although 'sometimes man look and say good', as the quaint style puts it. The next section hints at the external background ('In month of August to a cottage coming') but continues the obscurely-worded introspection about the growth of the individual and, in particular, the failure of love:

> So, insecure, he loves and love
> Is insecure, gives less than he expects.

108–9

However, by means of an inner activity described as 'the difficult work of mourning', the writer has hopes that the soul may be 'weaned at last to independent delight' and that finally at death we may find ourselves 'Not helplessly strange to the new conditions'. With a bit of puzzling one can follow Auden's thought, but it is hard to justify his clumsy exposition. The meanderings of introspection are difficult enough to follow without the added confusion of a guide speaking 'pidgin English'.

When the poem was reprinted in 1933 Auden omitted sixteen lines from the final section, and our prurient curiosity is naturally whetted when Beach tells us they contained vivid pictures of 'lusty youth struggling with the moral problem of sexual impulse'. The first banished passage seems to me mainly to be struggling to become comprehensible English:

> This is the account of growing, of knowing;
> First difference from first innocence
> Is feeling cold and nothing there,
> Continual weeping and oversleeping,
> Is mocking, nudging, and defence of fear;
> Verbal fumbling and muscle mumbling,
> Imagination by mispronunciation.
> Sebaceous belly, swollen skull,
> Exchanging hats and calling dear
> Are rich and silly, poor and dull.
>
> 143–52

The second deleted passage is no better as poetry, though it suggests more clearly the failure of sexual friendships:

> For this is how it ends,
> The account of growing, the history of knowing,
> As more comatose and always in,
> Living together in wretched weather
> In a doorless room in a leaking house,
> Wrong friends at the wrong time.
>
> 165–70

The decay in the social sphere is thus mirrored in personal relationships, and the imagery of the fourth section presents a décor of menace—suggestive rather than realistic. There is mention of 'storms', of the 'loud madman', of 'falling leaves', and the 'flooded football ground'. The technique resembles the Elizabethan device (now called the Pathetic Fallacy) of making tempests and natural prodigies reflect human tragedy (as does the storm in *King Lear*), but the modern reader, who does not believe in a correspondence between the human and the natural worlds, may ask why falling leaves or flooded football grounds should be portents of social revolution rather than mere signs of the approach of autumn. There is something theatrical and artificial in this device, because it is not now based on a genuine belief in the correspondence of the natural world with the human, and today we accept more easily Auden's image of children 'At play on the fuming alkali-tip' because we know that there are alkali-tips, and that they are not bits of figurative décor but true features of our industrial civilisation. Children really are menaced by alkali-tips, and the industrialisation they symbolise: they are not really menaced by falling leaves or storms.

The poem ends on a clear didactic note. The 'Tiny observer of enormous world' has abandoned his spectator's stance and now issues directions: 'It is time for the destruction of error.' The 'dragon' and the 'devourer' are summoned to purge society and human relationships of deep-seated ills. The style is both melodramatic and vague: 'To haunt the poisoned in his shunned house,/To destroy the efflorescence of the flesh . . .' The final lines once more return to the love-relationship theme, which merges with a condemnation of society. The decay, present both in personal love and in society, must suffer destruction, and there is a specific reference to the bourgeois régime as 'the old gang', with its symbolic 'hard bitch', the 'riding-master' and the 'lolling bridegroom'—not exactly, one would have thought, the most representative figures of bourgeois decadence. But, though we might find the underlying ideas here unconvincing, the poetry itself has a clarity and concreteness of image which impresses:

> We know it, we know that love
> Needs more than the admiring excitement of union . . .
> Needs death, death of the grain, our death,
> Death of the old gang . . .

The old gang to be forgotten in the spring,
The hard bitch and the riding-master,
Stiff underground; deep in clear lake
The lolling bridegroom, beautiful, there.

173–84

'JANUARY 1, 1931'

In 1930 Auden became a schoolmaster at Larchfield Academy, Helensburgh, Scotland, and the poem later entitled 'January 1, 1931' (first published in *The Orators*, 1932, as 'Ode I') retells a dream-vision after the style of the medieval poem *Piers Plowman*. The dreamer recalls an operation he underwent, at the same hour that D. H. Lawrence died, and gives glimpses of school-life with a colleague bending over the rain-gauge and the Headmaster 'gritting his teeth after breakfast' and quoting 'Call no man happy'. An undressed German rises from a lake, Stephen (Spender) signals from the sand dunes 'like a wooden madman', and Christopher (Isherwood) in wintry Europe

> . . . stood, his face grown lined with wincing
> In front of ignorance—'Tell the English,' he shivered,
>   'Man is a spirit.'

82–4

There are other topical references to people 'forgiving each other in the dark of the picture palaces'—Thirties poets often viewed cinemas suspiciously as escape routes into unreality—or, to unnamed individuals, such as the 'exile from superb Africa, employed in a laundry', and others who seem to be degenerates and 'self-regarders'. There are also various self-appointed 'healers' of society, dismissed contemptuously as:

> Of all the healers, Granny in mittens, the Mop, the white surgeon,
> And loony Layard.

One does not expect a dream to be very coherent, but should a poem about a dream be equally mystifying? In later editions of the poem Auden changed 'Stephen' to 'Pretzel' and 'Christopher' to 'Maverick', and replaced the nicknames of the healers with a slightly more respectful roll-call:

GA

97

> Granny in mittens, the Judge, the bucolic doctor,
> And the suave archdeacon.

But the poem remains hopelessly private in its allusions. One gathers that Auden and his friends consider themselves as radical reformers, aware of the dangers of Fascism, and it seems that news is awaited from Eastern Europe of the arrival of some mysterious champion who has 'thrown the bully of Corinth in the sanded circle' (which Beach suggests might mean Hitler). One can only contrast Auden's enigmatic prophecies with the explicit details in *Piers Plowman*, in which Langland tells us clearly that the King is going to come and beat the religious orders for breaking their rules, with a hearty blow specifically for the Abbot of Abingdon.

The idea of imitating Langland is piquantly original, and many of the lines are delightfully relaxed, with touches of unforced humour—'Far out in the water two heads discussed the position . . .' But the style wavers uneasily from the straightforward 'A train went clanking over the bridges' to the modern-medieval mixture of 'Felt sap collecting anon in unlighted cylinders . . .'. When Auden published the third edition of *The Orators* in 1966 his Foreword was mainly an apology for having written it at all. He does not mention this poem in particular, but he says of the volume itself:

> My name on the title-page seems a pseudonym for someone else, someone talented but near the border of sanity, who might well, in a year or two, become a Nazi . . . And over the whole work looms the shadow of that dangerous figure, D. H. Lawrence the Ideologue, author of . . . those sinister novels *Kangaroo* and *The Plumed Serpent* . . . In one of the Odes I express all the sentiments with which his followers hailed the advent of Hitler, but these are rendered, I hope, innocuous by the fact that the Führer so hailed is a new-born baby and the son of a friend.

So although critics have usually seen 'January 1, 1931' as an anti-Fascist poem, it is curious that Auden's own fears about the volume in which it appeared are that he was, at the time, being drawn towards a Nazi-like hero-worship. (Ode III, addressed to the new-born son of his friend Rex Warner, expresses crudely Auden's disgust with degenerate England. He says 'Mussolini, Pilsudski and Hitler have charm' though 'they make such a noise', and his picture of the proletariat is breezily superior:

> Fitters and moulders,
> Wielders and welders . . .
> Poofs and ponces,
> All of them dunces . . .
> Content for the year
> With food out of tins and very small beer . . .
> Spying on athletes playing on a green,
> Spying on kisses shown on a screen,
> Their minds as pathic as a boxer's face,
> Ashamed, uninteresting, and hopeless race.

One is not surprised at Auden's disgust, but whereas we might have expected a left-wing poet to say 'Let us liberate the proletariat from the deadening bourgeois drugs by building a healthy socialist society,' it is clear from the rest of the poem that he was falling into the Fascist attitude of 'These scum must be disciplined.')

'WHICH SIDE AM I SUPPOSED TO BE ON?'

The poem beginning 'Though aware of our rank . . .' was originally the fifth ode in *The Orators* (1932) and addressed 'To My Pupils'. In 1950 it was titled 'Which Side Am I Supposed to Be On?' without the dedication to pupils, but in 1966 it became merely 'Ode', and three stanzas were omitted—mainly passages which expand the details of military training and thus stress that the conflict will be bloody and relentless.

The local details are as vivid as a telegraphed newspaper report ('The agent clutching his side collapsed at our feet,/ "Sorry! They got me!" ') about which, however, a slight air of parody lingers. The military bric-à-brac of cocked pistols, code-words, unshaven agents, night-raids, bunting signals, and so on, is brilliantly suggestive of real warfare while at the same time injecting sardonic allusions to school training camps or *Boys'*

99

Best War Tales. It looks very much as though this ode was an exercise in irony, a tongue-in-cheek pep-talk by a conventional bourgeois schoolmaster who is urging his boys to prepare themselves for class-warfare against the dastardly Reds. Auden, of course, at this time was a 'revolutionary' schoolmaster, working within the reactionary system, and so his title 'Which Side Am I Supposed to Be On?' rather too obviously points to his dual role. If we read it, then, as an ironical attack on the bourgeois way of life, it is easy to distinguish the scorn for blind patriotism, religion prostituted to jingoism, and the repression of the pre-Christian pagan civilisation when there was an 'open wishing-well in every garden' and 'love came easy'. One stanza will illustrate how the irony is disguised as simulated praise for a religious ceremony which merely blesses the exultant bourgeois sport of class-warfare:

> Now we're due to parade on the square in front of the Cathedral,
> When the bishop has blessed us, to file in after the choir-boys,
> To stand with the wine-dark conquerors in the roped-off pews,
>> Shout ourselves hoarse:
> 'They ran like hares; we have broken them up like firewood;
>> They fought against God.'

37–42

But now Auden's technique of irony becomes elaborate—perhaps too elaborate. The Enemy, that is, Auden's side, the party of progress and enlightenment, is pictured as a 'scarecrow prophet', gathering at a limestone rift with his men, who tether their horses beside them like some marauding tribe (or the bad men in a Hollywood Western). His followers are none other than our old friends Fear, Wrath, Envy, Gluttony, Greed, Acedia and Lust, and although one can understand that the bourgeoisie is prone to ascribe all the Seven Deadly Sins to its political enemy, the very ingenuity of Auden's use of the allegorical method rather undermines his presentation of the progressive party. The Enemy's 'laconic war-bitten captain' has really been created by bourgeois fears. Their guerrillas have learnt from Wrath, and their 'brilliant pamphleteer' from Envy

It is true that the speaker is trying to denigrate the progressive party, but a certain ambiguity remains. Is Auden suggesting that in fact the progressives are utilising the evil instincts of man to beat the reactionaries, and that the progressives are only a psychological reaction to the puritanical, repressive, middle-class, Christian outlook? Auden's complicated irony is thus seen to be a Freudian-Marxist analysis of the progressive cause as described by a bourgeois schoolmaster using medieval Christian allegory. What, we might ask, is the point of such mental gymnastics? Only, I think, a clarification of either our knowledge of the bourgeois mind or of the whole process of class conflict. The bourgeois think the progressives are the Seven Deadly Sins incarnate, and Auden (and we) know that the bourgeois have created their enemy out of their own neuroses and ruling-class jingoistic, militaristic, church and school discipline system. (As Auden in an essay in 1934 said: 'The best reason I have for opposing Fascism is that at school I lived in a Fascist state . . .')

Many satirists have used the strategy of attacking the bourgeois system by pretending to be one of its spokesmen, and thus the reader is required to turn every remark on its head in order to appreciate the satirist's real viewpoint. This subversive, fifth-column technique is more subtle than a frontal attack, but if the satirist has to disguise himself as his enemy he sometimes runs the risk of ambiguity. Some critics have asserted that here, and in other poems, Auden secretly admires the system he is satirising. He may intend to expose the school discipline, its class code, its military training, and its manly sports, but he is half-attracted to them, and thus writes against them with an enjoyment which is too close to sympathy. Again, it has been said that the bourgeois system of repressions (sexual prudery, conventional behaviour, the public school code of honour, etc.) which Auden at this time condemned as chains upon the freedom of man, is not really all that different from the iron discipline (class solidarity, sexual purity, energetic political behaviour, etc.) demanded by Auden, and others, in the name of left-wing revolution. (One might parody Milton and say that 'New Discipline is but Old Repressions writ large'.) That is why in some of his early poems

Auden was able to use the manœuvres of the school Officers' Training Corps as a metaphor for left-wing militant struggle against the bourgeois system. In the 'Journal of an Airman', prose interspersed with poems, the presentation of a bourgeois rebel dedicated to the overthrow of society is rendered complicated and bewildering by the surrealistic parody of military attacks and social upheaval, and one ends by suspecting that revolution is really an absurd nightmare in the neurotic mind of a school-boy who has been hypnotised by Lawrence of Arabia. Here are some extracts to illustrate the flavour of this work:

> A main frontal attack. Divisions to be concentrated in the Shenly brick-fields and moved forward to the battle zone in bakers' vans, disguised as nuns . . . At 6 p.m. passages of unprepared translations from dead dialects are set to all non-combatants. The papers are collected at 6.10. All who fail to obtain 99 % make the supreme sacrifice. Candidates must write on three sides of the paper . . . Banks make payments in fairy gold; girl-guides, nocturnally stimulated, mob vicars at the climax of their sermons . . . at evensong choirs sing hymns in hesitation waltz time, form-masters find crude graffiti on their blackboards; the boys, out of control, imbibe Vimto through india-rubber tubing, openly pee into the ink-pots.

Here the Airman represents the disciplined, military attack of the progressives against a bourgeois society which collapses into absurd chaos. In 'Which Side Am I Supposed to Be On?', published in the same volume, it is the reactionary class which disciplines itself through military training, horse-riding, etc. But despite this rigorous programme the bourgeoisie is doomed, though in this poem Auden pictures its death as heroic, not surrealistically absurd:

> All leave is cancelled to-night; we must say good-bye.
> We entrain at once for the North; we shall see in the morning
> The headlands we're doomed to attack; snow down to the tide-line:
>   Though the bunting signals
> 'Indoors before it's too late; cut peat for your fires,'
>   We shall lie out there.

The question remains: can the revolutionary class-struggle be adequately presented in terms of Auden's Officers' Training Corps mythology? Is he not reducing a complex social process to the level of a romanticised vendetta, with not a little of the heroic atmosphere of the Icelandic sagas?

'A SUMMER NIGHT 1933'

Vega is the brightest star in the constellation Lyra (Greek for *lyre*) but its name is from an Arabic word meaning *falling*. I don't suppose Auden intended this esoteric allusion but it rather neatly suggests the theme of 'A Summer Night 1933' which opens with this stanza (in the more relaxed style of the 1936 volume, *Look, Stranger!*, in which it appeared):

> Out on the lawn I lie in bed,
> Vega conspicuous overhead
>   In the windless nights of June,
> As congregated leaves complete
> Their day's activity; my feet
>   Point to the rising moon.

The bright, but falling, moments which Auden celebrates in a delicate, lyrical fashion, are those calm evenings 'with colleagues in a ring' or the 'leisured drives through a land of farms' amid the 'sexy airs of summer'. This invocation of happy, tranquil friendships and simple, pleasant pursuits is also presented by means of a device which Auden becomes increasingly fond of—the ancient device of personification. There are modern touches (Fear carries a watch), and on the whole this is a welcome change from the polysyllabic abstractions which cluttered the earlier poems:

> The lion griefs loped from the shade
> And on our knees their muzzles laid,
>   And Death put down his book.

This congenial, private world of friendship, with its 'healers and the brilliant talkers./The eccentrics and the silent walkers', which includes also the 'tyrannies of love', endured with a sigh, is a falling world because it is threatened from the outside by violent forces. The tyrannies which cannot be endured with a sigh are political—there is a specific reference to Poland—and this reminds the poet that 'Our freedom in this English house,/ Our picnics in the sun' are only guaranteed by an unspecified 'doubtful act'. Two stanzas follow which express the disruptive danger from without in terms of a destructive flood which will force a rent through the 'dykes of our content'. The poet expresses a hope that the private delights he has known will somehow remain as potent forces to calm the 'pulse of nervous nations' and even 'forgive the murderer in his glass'.

The theme of the private world of delights, threatened by the public world of political turmoil, is no new one in literature. Indeed, in the 17th and 18th centuries, what one might call the Retreat Poem, in which the writer deliberately seeks a refuge from public strife in the innocent pleasure of a country house and garden, is more or less a genre in itself, stretching back at least as far as Horace, cosily sipping wine with friend or mistress on his Sabine farm. Marvell's 'The Garden' is probably the most famous meditation on this theme in the 17th century. Auden's Retreat Poem is striking because he does not close his eyes to the external threat: indeed he openly paints its horrors. Again we note a change in style. The earlier doom-charged images of sinister surgeons and bacteria-carrying agents are replaced by more traditional allusions to 'floods' and 'stranded monsters' which lie gasping on the black mud. However, floods can eventually 'make retreat' and so there is a guarded optimism about the ending, in which the poet affirms that the private life of personal delight is valid, is indeed 'tough' and patient enough to surpass the swiftness of the tigress.

The version of 'A Summer Night 1933', which we can now read in the 1950 or 1966 *Collected Shorter Poems*, is only three-quarters of the original poem. The deleted stanzas (5, 10, 11 and 12) carry personal references to intimate friendships and love which Auden no longer wishes to retain. Stanza 5 refers to the eyes of someone he can find with him in the morning when he wakes with the birds and the sun, and the other three stanzas speak of a hungry multitude, intruding upon his dream of private loves, and carry criticism of other people for their lack of achievement. He goes so far as to express his disillusion with members of Parliament and of Oxford University ('The Oxford colleges, Big Ben'), who have not met the challenges of the times. These omitted passages thus add both personal and political notes, and in particular speak sharply of some of his own friends who devote themselves to their own 'metaphysical distress' and make only a token gesture towards the large-scale problems of the day by showing 'kindness to ten persons'. These 'young radical' sentiments, and the rather erotic flavour of the recorded friendships between young men, may now not be to Auden's taste, but they seem to me to fit artistically into the general theme of the poem, and to make the private world, which he holds dear, more detailed, intimate, complex, credible—and less idealised.

'THE MALVERNS'

Another poem which has suffered at the hands of Auden's revising zeal is 'The Malverns', written when he was at the Downs School, Colwall, near Malvern, and first published in November 1933 in the *New Oxford Outlook*. When it was reprinted in *Look, Stranger!* in 1936, an eleven-line stanza was removed. In this he speaks of his guilty feelings at his uselessness in action, refers obliquely to D. H. Lawrence's connection with Nottinghamshire coal-mines, and alludes ironically to people he has previously taken for leaders. Perhaps 'the loony airman' is T. E. Lawrence, but it is not known who is meant by 'the little runt with Chaplains and a stock'. There is another unpleasant remark about the clergy, who are likened to the instincts which they had been told to follow and which Auden now says are

> Like corrupt clergymen filthy from their holes
> Deformed and imbecile.

In the 1945 *Collected Poetry* the whole poem was discarded, but in the 1950 *Collected Shorter Poems* four-fifths of it were restored. Seven stanzas in a row, in a different verse-form from the rest, were thus omitted, and they had included his recommendation of 'disciplined love' as a guide to the use of modern scientific forces, and the dogmatic statement that

> ... the major cause of our collapse
> Was a distortion in the human plastic by luxury produced.

In the 1966 *Collected Shorter Poems* the whole poem is again discarded. It would seem that though second thoughts are best, third thoughts are even better. Or will there be fourth thoughts in which the full 1933 version is restored to us?

Looking at the poem as it appears in the 1950 volume, we again have a fairly personal meditation about private happiness menaced by a political storm, although this time the period of delight has already passed and England now 'has no innocence at all'. From a characteristically elevated position, 'Aloof as admiral on the old rocks', Auden can see an express leaving eastward for a 'sailor's country', which he contrasts with 'the retired and rich' in Wales looking from 'the french windows of their sheltered mansions'. Perhaps the language of the first two stanzas is too relaxed and casual to mirror the poet's claim: 'I must have the truth', and the picture of poverty and economic collapse is ingeniously, but perhaps too playfully, based on a thin type of personification:

> Gross Hunger took on more hands every month,
> Erecting here and everywhere his vast
>   Unnecessary workshops,
> Europe grew anxious about her health,
> Combines tottered, credits froze,
> And business shivered in a banker's winter
>   While we were kissing.

27–33

We applaud Auden's desire to write vividly about unemployment and financial crises, but can the medieval device of personification really do the job? In turning these devastating impersonal forces into anxious invalids he has, I think, reduced their sinister and implacable character.

Once again, although Auden claims that he would like to be a 'digit of the crowd' and understand the ordinary people in shops and trams, he has none of that sympathetic acceptance of everyday human beings that we find in the work of Sean O'Casey, Brendan Behan or Dylan Thomas. The 'little men and their mothers' remain 'not plain but/Dreadfully ugly'. (This is hardly an advance on his dismissal of the workers as 'Poofs and ponces,/All of them dunces'.) This mood of revulsion is continued in his allusion to escapists in lanterned gardens, listening to saxophones 'moaning for a comforter', or surrendering to cinematic fantasies about noble robbers in Gaumont theatres. Equally escapist are the religious in their cathedrals ('Luxury liners laden with souls') in which they produce

> The high thin rare continuous worship
> Of the self-absorbed.   54-5

The cinema and the church are standard symbols of escapism for the left-wing (or right-wing) radicals of the Thirties, and we see that at this time Auden shared their views.

Next, in a review of European history which reminds us of the technique he is to use in 'Spain', Auden speaks of 'empires stiff in their brocaded glory' and of monasticism during 'ages of disorder'. The city civilisation of Ancient Greece is contrasted with the centralised state of Fascism by the use of the symbols of 'the delicate dove' and 'the hawk'. Totalitarian propaganda (and perhaps all kinds of propaganda) is summarised as speaking

> In the common language of collective lying,
> In codes of a bureau, laboratory slang
> And diplomats' French.   82-4

Once more using the Freudian concept of the Death Wish, Auden asserts that modern society is moribund:

> 'And all the customs your society has chosen
> Harden themselves into the unbreakable
> Habits of death,
> Has not your long affair with death
> Of late become increasingly more serious;
> Do you not find
> Him growing more attractive every day?'   90-6

The version we are studying does not include the trenchant, but surely oversimplified, diagnosis ('a distortion of the human plastic by luxury produced') and cure ('disciplined love'), and ends, as it began, on a personal note. Quoting Wilfred Owen and Katherine Mansfield, the poet is reminded by the Priory clock that he has to return to work, and he finishes with a quietly-voiced affirmation:

> These moods give no permission to be idle,
> For men are changed by what they do;
> And through loss and anger the hands of the unlucky
>   Love one another.
>
> 107–10

The argument of the poem is throughout blurred by obscure language and by phrases or words which may be thought insufficiently explicit. It is impossible for anyone but the poet to answer such questions as: what was the 'crime' the two friends were thinking of? what exactly is 'luscious lateral blossoming of woe' or 'angel assassins'? why do dividing cells raise the image of 'the reconciler'? what was the treasure, stolen and lost, which cannot be put back with caresses? This kind of muffled private language is in strong contrast to the bald assertions about 'luxury' and 'disciplined love', which Auden removed from the poem, together with such amateur psychological pronouncements as:

> Unable to endure ourselves, we sought relief
> In the insouciance of the soldier, the heroic sexual pose
> Playing at fathers to impress the little ladies . . .

The ending of the poem is positive, but vague. The poet is determined not 'to be idle' and he affirms that deeds change men, but the quotations from Wilfred Owen ('The poetry is in the pity') and from Katherine Mansfield ('To be rooted in life,/ That's what I want') indicate a sensitive humanism which is surely too general an antidote to the specific, historical and social diseases he has outlined. Is one correct in thinking that at this point Auden finds the world beyond cure and can therefore only think in terms of a personal salvation? The very last lines speak only of individual destiny and personal relationships:

> And through loss and anger the hands of the unlucky
>   Love one another.

The poem now titled 'Birthday Poem' and addressed to Christopher Isherwood is another work which has been in and out of the Auden canon. It was first printed in *New Verse* in 1935. In 1940 it appeared in the slim collection *Some Poems*, was eliminated from *Collected Poems*, 1945, surfaced once more in *Collected Shorter Poems* in 1950, only to submerge again by the time Auden issued the second *Collected Shorter Poems* of 1966. Presuming that a drowning poem rises three times there is some hope it may yet be rescued.

Again Auden contrasts an earlier carefree period of his life with the ominous present and future, and the allusions are largely autobiographical. This does not lead to obscure private references, however: the personal manner lends the poem a concreteness and an air of truth, counteracting the more general statements about Courage, Reason, Beauty and so on. Auden's talent for building a rapid picture out of telling details is seen in almost every stanza, and there are many memorable phrases such as 'The sallow oval faces of the city' or the image of holiday-makers entering cafés, wearing the 'tigerish blazer and the dove-like shoe'. This journalistic impressionism is very like the style of Louis MacNeice's poems of urban evocation, and Auden successfully presents the coach-trips, the yachting-outings, and the country-walks during summer vacations on the Isle of Wight, where amid popular entertainments (the 'complicated apparatus of amusement') the people can 'live their dreams of freedom'. The rather snobbish disapproval of ordinary people, noted elsewhere, is replaced by more indulgent criticism, for after all Auden had to some extent shared these pleasant moments. Despite his present rejection of the words of middle-class adolescents there is a certain nostalgic undertone when he recalls how, nine years before, as

> Half-boys, we spoke of books and praised
> The acid and austere, behind us only
> The stuccoed suburb and expensive school.   27–9

Even the make-believe, secret-agent atmosphere, which Auden

and Isherwood surrounded themselves with at university, is mocked fairly gently:

> Our hopes were set still on the spies' career,
> Prizing the glasses and the old felt hat,
> And all the secrets we discovered were
> Extraordinary and false . . .

33–6

Five summers later the two poets watch the 'Baltic from a balcony' and now they hope that 'love' is the solution to mankind's problems. They trust that 'one fearless kiss would cure/ The million fevers' (which sounds like oversimplified Freudian therapy) and that love might tame the 'dragon who had closed the works/While the starved city fed it with the Jews'. (It is not clear how far Auden sees this antidote to Nazi anti-semitism as part of their former immature beliefs.) At all events he is conscious of an earlier anti-bourgeois arrogance which could refuse 'The golf-house quick one and the rector's tea' and yet could surrender to the stupidity of 'private joking' or the sentimental lover's belief in 'the whisper in the double bed'. And so he asks 'Pardon for these and every flabby fancy'. Here, then, the idealisation of intimate friendships and love-affairs, seen in other poems of about the same period as potent forces for good, gives way to a realisation that they were immature poses amid a sheltered, middle-class environment. Now it is little comfort 'Among the well-shaped cosily to flit' while the wireless loudly roars its warnings and lies.

At this point the selfish vision of a boyhood protected by wealth and filled with an insubstantial fantasy life is challenged by the harsh reality of moral chaos and human injustice, and the 'close-set eyes of mother's boy' now see 'Scandal praying with her sharp knees up' and 'gaga Falsehood highly recommended'. The analysis of society is clothed in the allegorical style which Auden is now favouring. Sometimes the novelty of this device is effective, but the manufacture of capitalised vices and virtues does become rather facile and empty ('Reason stoned by Mediocrity'), which makes the vision of a harsh world in many ways less compelling than the vision of the pleasant escapist world:

> ... Smartness in furs,
> And Beauty scratching miserably for food,
> Honour self-sacrificed for Calculation,
> And Reason stoned by Mediocrity,
> Freedom by Power shockingly maltreated,
> And Justice exiled till Saint Geoffrey's Day.
>
> 75–80

The poem concludes with a call for Isherwood's 'strict and adult pen', in this hour of crisis and dismay, to expose the inadequacy of 'academy and garden', that is, the escapist world of intellectuals and suburban comforts, and to 'make action urgent and its nature clear'. Here the poet's call for *action*, expanded in the final stanza to suggest political action, makes this poem of 1935 nearer in tone to the 'Spain' of 1937. The last lines of the personal birthday poem, which had opened with August holiday scenes, close with ominous images of domestic music being silenced as man commits himself to the perilous torrents of history:

> In the houses
> The little pianos are closed, and a clock strikes.
> And all sway forward on the dangerous flood
> Of history, that never sleeps or dies,
> And, held one moment, burns the hand.
>
> 92–6

Perhaps today Auden feels this call to historical awareness, and resistance to 'savaging disaster', too theatrical or militant—one can only guess from his uncertainty about republishing the poem—but from a literary viewpoint it has a concreteness of image and lucidity of thought which have always made it attractive to readers. As a period piece, as evidence of the mood of a particular generation, it is without doubt revealing.

'SEPTEMBER I, 1939'

For many left-wing poets the 1930s had been a period of uncertainty, in which dreams of the death of the 'old gang' and the revolutionary transformation of society had gradually been changed into the nightmare of a resurgence of right-wing power.

It had emerged victorious in Spain, and then in 1939 the combined forces of Germany, Japan and Italy must have appeared to many to signal the proof of their worst fears. In January 1939 Auden and Isherwood left England to reside permanently in the United States, and Auden taught for a short time at St. Mark's School, Southborough, Massachusetts. About this time he wrote a pamphlet on education, contributed an essay to a collection entitled *I Believe*, gave lectures such as 'Democracy's Reply to the Challenge of Dictatorships' or 'Effective Democracy', reviewed a book on Voltaire under the heading 'A Great Democrat', and another book under the heading 'Democracy is Hard'. He also wrote a radio play called *The Dark Valley*. The impression is that Auden reacted to the war with positive activity in the field of educational and political ideas, striving to reach a wide public. About this time must date Auden's reassessment of his earlier beliefs and his acceptance of Christianity, though doubtless the process had been set in motion much before his move to America. Only Auden can know all the stages on this road to conversion. But the poem entitled 'September 1, 1939' affords us some evidence of his state of mind as he sat in 'one of the dives/On Fifty-Second Street' and pondered the meaning of the latest world disaster with its 'unmentionable odour of death'.

The short lines of laconic comment, often colloquial in style, but emphatic in rhythm, are very like the later poems of Yeats, and this adds to the impression that Auden is surveying with assurance the recent history of Europe, analysing the causes of the war and asserting what his own attitudes to the future will be. He begins by branding the Thirties as 'a low dishonest decade' and his explanation of why Germany has adopted Hitler as its 'psychopathic god' is a blend of Freudian, Marxist and Christian ideas. Auden is not explicit enough and tends to throw curt references at us with insufficient explication. He mentions 'Luther', presumably as the symbol of the subjection of Church to State Power. He alludes to 'what occurred at Linz', without telling us that this is where Hitler went to an Austrian *Realschule*. And so these shorthand-notes are not really expanded enough to enable us to agree with his conclusion that

> Those to whom evil is done
> Do evil in return.

21–2

This might refer only to the German nation's reactions to Lutheranism, or to Hitler's reaction to his schooling, or possibly to the current belief of the Thirties that Nazism was a product of a revengeful Versailles Treaty after the First World War. Whatever the value of Auden's ideas, we note that he is still indebted to Freudian psychology for his analysis of Hitler's school-induced psychopathic state, and to social historians for his conception of 'Statism' which has 'driven a culture mad'. As in his earlier poems the maladies of individuals and of state capitalism are seen as interlocking.

Auden's views remain Marxist enough to discover similar maladies in the American capitalist system, and his vocabulary still includes the terms 'imperialism' and 'competitive', though it is significant that his lines on 'Collective Man' voice fears rather than left-wing confidence. (For Auden an American skyscraper symbolises Collective Man rather than Collective Capitalists.)

> Into their neutral air
> Where the blind skyscrapers use
> Their full height to proclaim
> The strength of Collective Man,
> Each language pours its vain
> Competitive excuse . . .
> Out of the mirror they stare,
> Imperialism's face
> And the international wrong.

34–44

The New York bar, with its incessant music and electric lights, symbolises man's retreat from his true metaphysical state, which is likened to being

> Lost in a haunted wood,
> Children afraid of the night
> Who have never been happy or good.

53–5

This diagnosis of the human condition, as exhibited in a New York dive, seems to jump rather too eagerly to the general conclusion that a bar-room is symptomatic of the world at large, and in the next stanza Auden re-states an old conviction of his that self-love is 'true of the normal heart':

> For the error bred in the bone
> Of each woman and each man
> Craves what it cannot have,
> Not universal love
> But to be loved alone.   62–6

In earlier poems Auden had tried to define the nature of love. Sometimes he seemed to think of *Eros*, of Freudian libido, as a liberating force, though he saw it also acting as destructive self-love when frustrated (in particular in the lives of the neurotic bourgeoisie). Gradually Auden came to think of true love as *Agape*, the Christian idea of divine love, or love for others. I don't think that a study of Auden's poems reveals absolutely clear concepts of love. *Self-love, Eros, Agape* (and the terms themselves are capable of many interpretations) seem too much like ready-made concepts imported into poems, rather than conclusions arrived at by the poet after due examination of human behaviour. But it seems safe to say that Auden's initial 'Freudian' exultation in sexual love as a means of freeing the individual from bourgeois chains gave way to a suspicion that this was only self-love in a new guise. And thus in the next stanza he is able to accuse romantic and sexual escapism, as well as political authoritarianism, of being *lies*. I quote this stanza in full because it was deleted by Auden in the *Collected Poems* of 1950.

> All I have is a voice
> To undo the folded lie,
> The romantic lie in the brain
> Of the sensual man-in-the-street
> And the lie of Authority
> Whose buildings grope the sky:
> There is no such thing as the State
> And no one exists alone;

> Hunger allows no choice
> To the citizen or the police;
> We must love one another or die.

It has been suggested that Auden removed this stanza because
the last line was too trite, or because his attack on Authority and
State might lead us to suppose him an anarchist. I would guess
that Auden now dislikes the argument of the last three lines,
which say, in effect, that both ordinary people and the coercive
police authority are compelled to love each other by forced
hunger, i.e. sheer economic necessity. As a reading of history this
seems manifestly over-simple, and for a Christian the 'love' which
is compulsorily born out of economic determinism could hardly
be more than a selfish desire to survive. One can understand
Auden's deletion of the stanza: one cannot congratulate him on
his facile pronouncements on complex matters.

The poem ends (not surprisingly when one considers its title)
in massive despair illuminated by a few sparks of hope. One
notes that there is no reference to the role of mass movements or
even groups of people. It looks as though 'the Just' are composed
of isolated individuals who can do little more than exchange
messages:

> Defenceless under the night
> Our world in stupor lies;
> Yet, dotted everywhere,
> Ironic points of light
> Flash out wherever the Just
> Exchange their messages:
> May I, composed like them
> Of Eros and of dust,
> Beleaguered by the same
> Negation and despair,
> Show an affirming flame.

78–88

One can sympathise with the mood of 'Negation and despair',
and most people react favourably, I suppose, to the cautious
optimism. Opinions will differ as to who the 'Just' are, and
how helpful their messages will prove without popular support

of some kind. Since Auden has already exposed the lies or weak-nesses of Luther, Hitler, Germans, Collective Man, Imperialism, commutors, governors, bar habitués, man-in-street, Author-ity, State, citizens and police, one does rather wonder who is left to compose the Just. In earlier poems he had seemingly condemned bourgeois society wholesale, as neurotic and socially sterile, pinning his hopes however on progressive forces. Now the condemnation is even more widespread: it is Man himself (including Auden) who is composed of 'Eros and of dust'. The division into the 'old gang' and those who, in 'Spain', supported the 'struggle' has disappeared. A possible way out of this impasse would be a faith in good people, good causes, and good move-ments, wherever they exist, within or outside any particular system. I cannot see that 'the Just' implies such a faith. At all events the word itself, in its present context, remains vague. One can only speculate about Auden's present views on this poem, but in the *Collected Shorter Poems* of 1966 it was dropped completely, though it remains one of his best-known poems because it features in many anthologies of modern verse.

'CHRISTMAS 1940'

'September 1, 1939' reveals Auden's increasing interest in a relig-ious view of life and, as we might expect, many poems of the war years are preoccupied with theological ideas and a personal quest for faith. In 'Christmas 1940' (which is surprisingly dropped in the 1966 collection) Auden experiences despair at the vision of a meaningless world of chance events:

> How can the mind make sense, bombarded by
> A stream of incompatible mishaps,
> The bloom and buzz of a confessed collapse?

6–8

The style varies from colloquialism to philosophical abstractions, with an occasional use of the familiar device of personification (if that's the right word for an animal): 'The lion of Nothing chases about.' But on the whole the abstract style dominates, even in the rapid sketch of the history of life on our planet.

The catalogue technique of 'Spain' and other poems of the Thirties is now replaced by rather difficult passages of scientific or philosophical commentary upon roses or fish:

> Through a long adolescence, then, the One
> Slept in the sadness of its disconnected
> Aggressive creatures—as a latent wish
> The local genius of the rose protected,
> Or an unconscious irony within
> The independent structure of the fish . . .

31–6

This is ambitious verse in which Auden is striving to present a religious conception of evolution in the form of poetry. The manipulation of profound ideas gives us here a glimpse of the intellectual anxieties which lie behind Auden's conversion to Christianity, and one can only applaud his attempt to compel such difficult material into poetic mould. But the thought *is* difficult and the language near to text-book abstraction. He is more successful where he can marry abstract ideas to concrete expression, as in these lines on the breakdown of ancient religious frameworks of belief in an ordered universe (as expressed in Greek animism, astrology, etc.):

> The sacred auras fade from well and wood,
> The great geometries enclose our lives
> In fields of normal enmity no more . . .
> Venus cannot predict our passion, nor
> The Dioscuri plant their olive trees
> To guide us through the ambiguities.

49–56

Auden concludes that man now exists in a seemingly absurd, chance universe, 'reduced to our true nakedness', and we must either serve 'some Hitlerian monster' or submit ourselves to the 'Unconditional'—his term for God. Everybody, 'beggar, bigwig, mugwump', can have some 'vision of that holy centre where/All time's occasions are refreshed' and thereby our problems are solved. Auden's social and political creed is now no longer the radical demand for the extinction of the old by the new, but a programme of Christian reconciliation. I think many readers will find the attitudes a little too like the easy optimism of Moral Rearmament, and one does ask what the following phrases really imply in actual practice:

> ... the lost
> Are met by all the other places there,
> The rival errors recognise their love,
> Fall weeping on each other's neck at last;
> The rich need not confound the Persons, nor
> The Substance be divided by the poor.

67–72

Again Auden uses the word *love* to designate the only power that can save mankind, and one has to assume that it is *Agape*, Christian love, that is meant. The final stanza stresses man's free choice of heaven or hell, the unique force of love in an absurd world, and the ability of faith to understand one's destiny:

> Our way remains, our world, our day, our sin;
> We may, as always, by our own consent
> Be cast away: but neither depth nor height
> Nor any other creature can prevent
> Our reasonable and lively motions in
> This modern void where only Love has weight,
> And Fate by Faith is freely understood,
> And he who works shall find our Fatherhood.

81–8

Whatever one may think of the Christian ideas re-stated here, from a literary viewpoint the poetry is disappointing. Language such as 'neither depth nor height/Nor any other creature' (borrowed from St. Paul) is colourless and banal. Perhaps in an attempt to provide a simple, untheatrical ending to a rather complicated argument, Auden has given us something nearly as trite as a hymn. (The deliberately flat style of poems of this period seems partly the influence of Eliot's *Four Quartets*. In 'Autumn 1940', now re-titled 'The Dark Years', the resemblance to Eliots' characteristic language makes Auden's poem read like pastiche:

> time remembered bear witness to time required,
> the positive and negative ways through time
> embrace and encourage each other
> in a brief moment of intersection . . .)

61–4

From now on we may expect Auden's 'poetic manifestos' to be Christian, though as usual he will surprise us with new styles, and the rather conventional expression of belief gives way to unusual experiments in presentation—including religious light verse. (He has not yet rewritten the *Book of Job* in the form of limericks, but one feels he might very well do so.)

'UNDER WHICH LYRE'

In some of his Thirties poems Auden had posed as a bourgeois figure, thus obliquely satirising society by allowing his *persona* to reveal its own social backwardness. In 'Under Which Lyre: A Reactionary Tract for the Times' (which was his Phi Beta Kappa poem at Harvard for 1946) Auden disarmingly claims to be supporting a reactionary attack on the orthodox American ideals of collectivism and conformism. To be reactionary, in the modern American context, is to remain an individualist, to refuse to kowtow to Science or Commercialised Art or Bureaucracy. The poem is of course written for a university campus and perhaps one should not expand the significance of the witty stanzas such as this one, which describes the return of ex-service-men to English Department tutorials:

> Among bewildering appliances
> For mastering the arts and sciences
>   They stroll or run,
> And nerves that steeled themselves to slaughter
> Are shot to pieces by the shorter
>   Poems of Donne.

13–18

Auden divides men into followers of Apollo, who run the world, and the sons of Hermes (like himself) who follow their own bent. So, whereas the 'sons of Hermes love to play', the children of pompous Apollo 'never shrink/From boring jobs but have to think/Their work important'. He likens this eternal quarrel between the two types to the confrontation of 'Falstaff the fool' and the 'prig Prince Hal'. Auden suggests also that the opposition is that of 'the heart' versus 'common sense', and that Apollo's 'official art' and utilitarian education system have conquered the American academic scene:

> And when he occupies a college,
> Truth is replaced by Useful Knowledge;
>   He pays particular
> Attention to Commercial Thought,
> Public Relations, Hygiene, Sport,
>   In his curricula.

79–84

Apollo's success can be seen on Broadway, in book reviews, in radio commercials, in the sexy novels written by co-eds, and even in existentialist writers (for they are only Apollo soldiers in fake Hermes uniforms). Still speaking largely in terms of academic affairs Auden composes a Hermetic Decalogue, or ten commandments, against various orthodox sins:

> Thou shalt not answer questionnaires
> Or quizzes upon World-Affairs,
>   Nor with compliance
> Take any test. Thou shalt not sit
> With statisticians nor commit
>   A social science.

157–62

The positive advice offered in the final lines is in keeping with the bantering tone of the poem:

>   If thou must choose
> Between the chances, choose the odd;
> Read *The New Yorker*, trust in God;
>   And take short views.

171–4

As the title of the poem suggests, Auden is aware that his views must seem those of an old-fashioned individualist, an 'unpolitical' nonconformist, who prefers to be eccentric and pragmatic rather than accept the pseudo-scientific, commercialised, over-organised, mass-produced culture of modern America. Auden's attitudes are not specially original—the Individualist has been fighting a rearguard action against Society for a long time—but one suspects that they are now stiffened by his religious concern for an individual privacy which cannot be invaded by social conformist forces. It is interesting to realise that a Soviet poet, for instance, could attack 'socialist bureaucracy' in much the same terms as an American poet can attack capitalist uniformitarianism. Moreover, if we consider Auden's early verse, in which he advocated a 'Freudian' and 'Marxist' liberation from bourgeois puritanical conformism and economic exploitation, we can see that his concern for individual *freedom from systems* has remained, though the actual context of struggle has changed. This is not to say that 'Under Which Lyre' is a Marxist or Freudian onslaught on American capitalist culture. He does say, fairly pleasantly, 'Thou shalt not be on friendly terms/With guys in advertising firms', but his main criticism centres on scientific utilitarianism, over-efficient administration, bad novels and poems. One is reminded of Alexander Pope satirising butterfly-collectors and literary dunces rather than of the piercing analysis of Freud or Marx. One cannot say that Auden has forsaken Freudian-Marxism for Christian Individualism, for the Freudian-Marxist critique of society never entered very profoundly into his work. Even in his 'left-wing' verse Auden shows little, if any, awareness of proletarian suffering. He does speak frequently of the sick bourgeoisie and the collapsed bourgeois economy, but the deserted mines and rusting machinery of his earliest verse reflect bankrupt industry, not the agonies of the unemployed. Today, more radical critics of the American system than Auden are the beatniks (who would not be seen dead at a Harvard campus ceremony) or the protest-groups who would be occupying buildings or possibly setting fire to them. There is nothing in Auden's poem which suggests violent or even active opposition to conformism, for although the imagery is military, the actual warfare is academically pedantic:

> Lone scholars, sniping from the walls
> Of learned periodicals,
>   Our facts defend,
> Our intellectual marines,
> Landing in little magazines
>   Capture a trend.

133–8

But when Auden wrote in 1940 that 'Thou shalt not do as the dean pleases' or 'bow down before/Administration', he could hardly have foreseen that, some twenty years later, militant students would in fact capture the Harvard administration building and eject the deans. One wonders whether he approves of the militant students who have followed his 'reactionary' advice. (Stephen Spender, incidentally, has recently (1969) published an investigation into student unrest.)

'A WALK AFTER DARK'

When one recalls the early 'manifestos' of inner conflict, in which Auden was very conscious of the opposition between the happy personal life of himself and his Oxford friends, and the bitter problems posed by society or political events, it is interesting to turn to such a poem as 'A Walk After Dark', the last poem in the volume *Nones* (1951). (It had been published in 1949 and seemingly composed before 1948, according to *Collected Shorter Poems* (1966), where it now can be most easily found.) We remember that one summer evening in 1933 he had contemplated the bright star Vega: now he begins on a romantic note as he watches the cloudless night which can 'set the spirit soaring'. But this mood quickly changes to disillusionment as he realises that since Newton the world has become for us a dead machine, replacing the spirit-peopled universe of earlier periods:

> The clockwork spectacle is
> Impressive in a slightly boring
> Eighteenth-century way.

This intellectual *ennui* is paralleled by his middle-aged feeling of being 'unready to die/But already at the stage/When one starts to dislike the young', and he takes refuge in a make-believe universe, though the word 'cosier' shows he doesn't really take it seriously:

> It's cosier thinking of night
> As more of an Old People's Home
> Than a shed for a faultless machine...
>
> 19–21

However, he rejects the stoic manner of classical authors and the '*lacrimae rerum* note' which, he says somewhat cynically, you can only strike if you are young or rich. Auden regards stoic resignation as a pose. He insists on recognising both the harsh nature of reality and man's own responsibility for it:

> For the present stalks abroad
> Like the past and its wronged again
> Whimper and are ignored,
> And the truth cannot be hid;
> Somebody chose their pain,
> What needn't have happened did.
>
> 31–6

He does not mention what are these particular wrongs (presumably about 1947) or which ominous 'event may already have hurled' itself against our 'laws'. The terms are far too vague and one would like to know whether he is referring to atomic extinction of humanity, or what—it could mean almost anything. This vagueness makes the ending seem melodramatically sombre, reminding us of the very early Auden poems of menacing and mysterious doom:

> As I walk home to bed,
> Asking what judgment waits
> My person, all my friends,
> And these United States.
>
> 45–8

The insistence on an individual responsibility for human suffering is diluted by the inarticulate pessimism of the ending. One can understand the writer's mood, but one asks whether a brooding anxiety is any better than the *lacrimae rerum* note or the impressive, if boring, 18th-century response to a mechanical universe. The Christian sensitivity to suffering, and recognition of personal responsibility for it, seem too weak to survive the anguish of uncertainty about the future. The term 'judgment', in the lines above, is also too imprecise. Is it history's judgment on the political role of the U.S., or God's judgment on the sins of its citizens? What has happened to the policy of 'trust in God;/And take short views'? What one criticises in this poem is not the Christian approach but the lack of it. *Anguish* may well be in the Christian's vocabulary, but must he not reject *despair*?

'VESPERS'

In his essay 'Dingley Dell and the Fleet' (collected in *The Dyer's Hand*, 1963), in which he declares that the real theme of *Pickwick Papers* is the Fall of Man, Auden explains at some length his distinction between 'the Arcadian whose favourite daydream is of Eden, and the Utopian whose favourite daydream is of New Jerusalem'. The motto over the gate of Eden is 'Do what thou wilt is here the Law', whereas the New Jerusalem motto is 'In His Will is our peace'. We have met the Arcadians and Utopians before in the light-hearted Harvard poem 'Under Which Lyre'. They appear again in the prose-poem 'Vespers', published in 1955 in *The Shield of Achilles*. 'Vespers' is the fifth poem in the sequence called *Horae Canonicae*, which comprises seven poems in different metres and style based on the canonical hours and the associated offices of the church. These daily offices celebrate historical events relating to the Crucifixion.

Much of the humour of the earlier treatment is retained and expanded, though the amusing paragraphs are counter-balanced by sombre ones. The poet, who is an Arcadian, imagines that in the twilight he meets his Anti-type, a Utopian, and the poem proceeds with a series of contrasts:

He would like to see me cleaning latrines: I would like to see him
  removed to some other planet.

Glancing at a lampshade in a store window, I observe it is too
  hideous for anyone in their senses to buy: he observes it is too
  expensive for a peasant to buy.

In Auden's Eden people like Bellini play with obsolete saddle-
tank locomotives, listen to gossip, observe compulsive rituals
and superstitious taboos, but have no morals. In the Utopian's
New Jerusalem people are obliged to like work, even 'chefs will
be cucumber-cool machine minders', there will be 'a special
daily lesson in simplified spelling for non-verbal types', and all
will 'practise the rational virtues' although the 'temples will be
empty'.

The contrasts are deliberately amusing, excessive, and pushed
to the point of intellectual farce, as in the deadpan grotesquer-
ies of *Gulliver's Travels* or some modern *New Yorker* satire,
and the tone of super-sophisticated fun makes 'Vespers' an
original contribution to Christian meditation. One must be
grateful to Auden for thus expanding the range of religious
verse.

We may think that Auden's division of certain people into
Arcadians and Utopians is too simple, and thus his declaration
of their eternal antipathy both pessimistic and unnecessary. If
between them 'no treaty is negotiable', at least he does recognise
that each is somehow a part of the other: perhaps they are really
'two accomplices' each 'loyal to different fibs'. Here the initial
clarity of the contrasting types is exchanged for a notion of two
necessary visions which correct each other. Each accomplice
is able 'to remind the other (do both, at bottom, desire truth?)
of that half of their secret which he would most like to forget'.
At this point, and only late in the poem, is a specific reference
made to the Crucifixion. The Arcadian and the Utopian face
each other and force each other 'to remember our victim (but
for him I could forget the blood, but for me he could forget the
innocence)'. The final lines conclude with this assertion about the
'victim':

on whose immolation (call him Abel, Remus, whom you will, it is one Sin Offering) arcadias, utopias, our dear old bag of a democracy are alike founded:

For without a cement of blood (it must be human, it must be innocent) no secular wall will safely stand.

The Arcadian and the Utopian, says Auden, are united in their guilt: all systems, including the 'dear old bag of a democracy' (one notes the affectionate abuse), are founded on the sacrificial killing of Christ, whose human and innocent blood guarantees the validity of everything secular. One suspects that the need to include a reference to the Crucifixion in this Christian meditation has obliged Auden to contrive a religious, harmonious ending to the imagined hostilities he has so amusingly pictured between himself and his Anti-type. The 'unity in guilt' device, and the rather unclear argument that secular systems are somehow made to stand safely through Christ's sacrificial death, are not very convincing to me. One has to ask, quite simply: are human beings divided into Arcadian and Utopian; do they confront each other and remind each other of their mutual guilt; does this cause them to remember Christ; are Arcadias, Utopias and democracies founded on this immolation? In other words, has Auden's meditation at the hour of vespers enabled him to penetrate deeply into Christian wisdom, or do his original and provocative words merely reflect a wishful desire to reconcile contradictory tendencies in human thought under the unifying symbol of the Crucifixion? There is an advance on 'Under Which Lyre' in that Auden, formerly proud of being an Arcadian, here reveals the weaknesses of his position ('Passing a slum child with rickets, I look the other way,' or 'we have no morals') and is willing to share the mutual guilt for Christ's death. Is it unfair to suggest that the conflict between the Bellini-loving Arcadian and the scientific Utopian (whose ideal becomes, in practice, a 'day of outrage when hellikins cavort through ruined drawing-rooms') is but another way of expressing the older conflict within Auden of the cultured bourgeois and the urgent left-wing radical? If this be true, then we can see that this conflict is still present in a different guise in his later verse, and that the tendency now is to find a solution to it in terms of Christianity. The bourgeois Auden must recognise his radical conscience, and the reformist Auden must recognise the cultural heritage of capitalism. The slum child must be cured of rickets and be able to enjoy Bellini or the bellowing 'from the Cathedral (romanesque) of St. Sophie'.

No doubt Auden will continue to issue 'manifestos' of the kind we have been studying, and we remain grateful for the energy and technical versatility which inform this poetic genre, with its fusion of 'confessional' self-revelation and concern for social and philosophical issues.

5

Longer Works

One has the impression that the modern poet is, as Théophile Gautier diagnosed, '*de courte haleine*', and that the typical piece of verse today consists of a dozen terse lines, not infrequently jammed between the end of a short story and the advertisement for the latest American text-book in a little magazine ('Poems must not exceed 24 lines,' says the editor of *Ariel* in 1969). The long poem is not easy to get published; the Imagist movement and the influence of the brief Japanese forms may also have discouraged the more expansive sorts of poems. Another of Auden's virtues is his strenuous attempt to write longer works, and within this field he has also provided us with an inventive range of genres—the verse-and-prose journal (in *The Orators*, 1932), the chatty Byronic travel-book (in *Letters from Iceland*, 1937), the topographical-philosophical sonnet-sequence and verse commentary inspired by the visit to China (in *Journey to a War*, 1939), the reflective letter-poem in rhymed octosyllabics published with *The Quest* sonnet-sequence (in *New Year Letter*, 1941), the verse-and-prose commentary on Shakespeare's *The Tempest*, called *The Sea and the Mirror* and printed with the 'Christmas Oratorio' *For the Time Being* (1944), and the 'baroque eclogue' entitled *The Age of Anxiety* (1948). Some of these works are semi-dramatic and remind us of Auden's plays written in collaboration with Christopher Isherwood: *The Dog Beneath the Skin* (1935), *The Ascent of F6* (1936), *On the Frontier* (1938). Auden also wrote two verse-plays, before collaborating with Isherwood: *Paid on Both Sides* (1930) and *The Dance of Death* (1933).

It is not possible in this study to examine all these lengthy works with the care they deserve and no doubt for most readers the shorter poems will remain of primary interest. Some of the sonnets and songs from the volumes noted above have been reprinted in *Collected Shorter Poems*, but the plays have seldom been revived on the stage. The earliest verse-drama, *Paid on Both Sides*, has been praised highly by Professor Empson and others. It is in many ways a fascinating experiment and short enough to be dealt with in some detail.

'PAID ON BOTH SIDES'

The charade, *Paid on Both Sides*, written in 1928 when Auden was 21, was included in *Poems* (1930) and has been reprinted in other collections. In its twenty-seven pages and through its twenty-nine characters, which range from The Spy to Father Xmas, not to mention The Chorus, Auden tells the story of a murderous blood-feud between two northern families. The plot, to adapt the old cliché, does not thicken but rather hides behind difficult passages of verse and dodges about between wildly differing scenes—a few of the stage directions will give some idea of the surrealist atmosphere of the play:

> Back curtains draw. Joan with child and corpse . . .
> Enter Father Christmas. He speaks to the audience . . .
> The Man-Woman appears as a prisoner of war behind barbed wire, in the snow . . .
> Doctor takes circular saws, bicycle pumps, etc., from his bag . . .
> Spy behind a gate guarded by Xmas . . .
> Gramophone. A dance. As the dance ends, the back curtains draw and the Butler enters centre . . .
> A shot. More shots. Shouting . . .

The two households, the Nowers and the Shaws, are mill-owners in, presumably, the north of England, but they and their workmen are engaged in a blood-feud similar to those pictured in the medieval Icelandic sagas, and this private warfare from generation to generation is accepted as part of their daily life. John Nower, whose father's murder caused his mother to give birth to him prematurely, falls in love with Anne Shaw and wishes to marry her, which would end the feud. John has, however, already killed Anne's brother in revenge for his father's death, and so at the marriage-feast Anne's mother persuades a second son to kill John Nower, and the feud resumes. Dick, a close friend of John, leaves for the Colonies.

Some of the scenes are fairly straightforward accounts of ambushes and military preparations:

> Let me see the map. There's a barn about a hundred yards from the house. Yes, here it is. If we can occupy that without attracting attention it will form a good base for operations, commands both house and road. p. 11

Murder has become so routine that it can be easily discussed over drinks as a topic equally interesting as sport. Here the naturalistic prose disarmingly presents the horror beneath the seemingly innocent conversation:

> W. Two half pints, Zeppel, please. (*To Kurt*). Can you let me have a match? How is the Rugger going?
> K. All right, thank you. We have not got a bad team this season.
> W. Where do you play yourself?
> K. Wing 3 Q.
> W. Did you ever see Warner? No, he'd be before your time. You remember him don't you, Trudy?
> T. He was killed in the fight at Colefangs, wasn't he?
> W. You are muddling him up with Hunter. He was the best three-quarter I have ever seen. His sprinting was marvellous to watch. p. 12

For other effects Auden devised a clipped, concentrated verse style, suggested by the Icelandic or Anglo-Saxon sagas, which matches the abrupt harshness of violence:

> Shot answered shot Bullets screamed
> Guns shook Hot in the hand
> Fighters lay Groaning on ground
> Gave up life Edward fell
> Shot through the chest First of our lot
> By no means refused fight Stephen was good
> His first encounter Showed no fear
> Wounded many. p. 15

By deleting pronouns or grammatical connective words Auden produces a stark verse which seems appropriate to the action and the mood, but when done to excess the effect is of stuttering phrases jammed together, of verbal congestion and artificiality, often leading to obscurity:

> Can speak of trouble, pressure on men
> Born all the time, brought forward into light
> For warm dark moan.
> Though heart fears all heart cries for, rebuffs with mortal beat
> Skyfall, the legs sucked under, adder's bite.   p. 8

There are several long, reflective speeches in which the futility of the feud, the basic inhumanity of man, or the conflicts in the minds of the main characters are presented, and here the play deals with the seemingly permanent features of the human condition. The moods of despair and the fugitive signs of hope could equally be those of the sagas or of modern man:

> Sometimes we read a sign, cloud in the sky,
> The wet tracks of a hare, quicken the step
> Promise the best day. But here no remedy
> Is to be thought of, no news but the new death;
> A Nower dragged out in the night, a Shaw
> Ambushed behind the wall. Blood on the ground
> Would welcome fighters. Last night at Hammergill
> A boy was born fanged like a weasel. I am old,
> Shall die before next winter, but more than once shall hear
> The cry for help, the shooting round the house.   p. 13

In other sections the modern references are quite deliberately stressed, and we are thus made to reflect upon contemporary social and industrial matters:

> The Spring unsettles sleeping partnerships,
> Foundries improve their casting process, shops
> Open a further wing on credit till
> The winter. In summer boys grow tall
> With running races on the froth-wet sand,
> War is declared there, here a treaty signed ...   p. 17

The boldest technical experiment occurs about the middle of the play, after John has ordered the spy to be shot. Father Christmas enters and speaks chummily to the audience, introducing a section of surrealist farce (not unlike the less grim German Expressionist plays or some of the recent absurdist drama, such as Ionesco's). The stage direction reads: '*A trial. John as the accuser. The Spy as accused. Joan as his warder with a gigantic feeding-bottle. Xmas as president, the rest as jury, wearing school caps.*' The dialogue is a mixture of serious verse, especially from a character called *Man-Woman* who appears as a prisoner-of-war behind barbed wire, and of slapstick humour from a peculiar *Doctor:*

[*Enter Doctor and his Boy.*]
B. Tickle your arse with a feather, sir.
D. What's that?
B. Particularly nasty weather, sir.   p. 21

The Doctor extracts a large tooth from the body of the Spy, who arises and is snapped by a Photographer. John and the Spy finally plant a tree together and speak enigmatically in verse. Professor William Empson claimed in 1931: 'But at the crisis, when John has just ordered the Spy to be shot, a sort of surrealist technique is used to convey his motives. They could only, I think, have been conveyed in this way, and only when you have accepted them can the play be recognised as a sensible and properly motivated tragedy.'

I can only say that for me the dialogue and actions in this scene remain impenetrably obscure, though I think I catch a glimpse of a Freudian explanation of John's motives from the feeding-bottle, the tooth, and some of the sexual phrases used by the Man-Woman.

However, looking at the play as a whole, it is possible to discern a psychological level of meaning. Mothers fairly obviously have a bad influence on their children, for Joan vows over the corpse of her husband that John will continue the feud, and it is Seth Shaw's mother who makes him ambush the wedding-group. As the Chorus says finally: 'His mother and her mother won.' In the surrealistic episode Joan threatens the spy with her enormous feeding-bottle, shouting: 'Be quiet, or I'll give you a taste of this.' All this may or may not be good psychology, but is it good literature?

As in other works Auden again seems to wish to marry Freud and Marx. Perhaps a more important level in this charade is the political one. This was clearly recognised and applauded by some critics in the Thirties. Empson spoke of the play being about 'the problems involved in the attempt to change radically a working system'. Edwin Berry Burgum in a review (collected in the American anthology *Proletarian Literature*) analysed the play as 'an attempt to vivify the waste and barbarism of capitalistic competition by personifying it . . . What method could be more vivid than picturing the family life of the capitalist in conjunction with his business methods? He has only to assume the old situation when the owner lived near his mill and add to it the methods of violence practised under modern expansion. The capitalist is then clearly disclosed as a feudal brigand in constant guerrilla warfare upon his neighbouring capitalistic opponents . . . And at the end a younger son migrates to the colonies to symbolise the development of imperialistic capitalism.' (In 1963 Monroe K. Spears, in *The Poetry of W. H. Auden*, interprets Dick's migration as 'changing one country for another. . . giving allegiance to the Marxist society of the future'.)

There may be disagreement about detailed interpretation of the political allegory but Auden's general intention to portray the intrinsic violence of capitalist society does not seem to be in doubt. His brilliant idea of a pokerfaced presentation of modern life as identical with medieval tribal feuding seems to me the most remarkable thing about *Paid on Both Sides*, and an unexpected use of his study of the ancient sagas. (It is interesting to note his comment on them in his *Letters from Iceland*, 1937: 'I love the sagas, but what a rotten society they describe, a society with only the gangster virtues.') What a pity that Auden lessened the impact of his brilliant idea by wrapping it in such difficult verse. And the uncertainty about the interpretation of Dick's migration leaves the political meaning of the play ambiguous. The final Chorus hesitates between a general pessimistic moral ('Though he believe it, no man is strong') and what seems like advice to the young to leave the old, corrupt society ('let the son/Sell the farm lest the mountain fall'). Obscurity and ambiguity have, it seems to me, marred this play. One does not of course ask Auden for the facile, black-and-white oversimplifications of propaganda drama but rather for the profound clarity which one finds in Sophocles or Shakespeare. This may be asking a lot of a writer of twenty-one but in literary criticism one cannot make any concessions for age.

'THE DANCE OF DEATH'

Reference to *The Orators* is made elsewhere in this study and so we may pass to a consideration of *The Dance of Death*, acted in 1933 at the Group Theatre. It is not so much a play as a didactic revue. Auden himself said in the programme note: 'The music hall, the Christmas pantomime, and the country house charade are the most living drama of today.' It is difficult to assess the play from the text because it appears thin when divided from theatrical devices—jazz orchestra on stage, musical-comedy chorus, actors planted in the audience, actors miming scenery, songs, dances, etc. The Announcer states the theme at the outset:

> We present to you this evening a picture of the decline of a class, of how its members dream of a new life, but secretly desire the old, for there is death inside them. We show you that death as a dancer.

The plot, such as it is, involves the Chorus of jazz-generation fun-lovers, whose clothes are stolen, donning the costumes from a 1916 musical revue. The hit number is 'Soldiers of the King of Kings' and somehow the mood changes to one of militant Marxism. The Manager is perturbed, not unnaturally, and employs the Dancer to divert them. He is a fusion of saviour, hero, mystic, and Fascist demagogue, who rouses the crowd to a wild pitch of Nazi-type nationalism, but the Ship of State runs on to the rocks and the Dancer-Führer falls unconscious. When revived he appears to have turned his thoughts to meditation and mysticism. Amid some final festivities the Dancer dies, his demise being pronounced by no less a person than Karl Marx (whose ludicrous entry reminds one more of Groucho Marx than the political theorist Auden at this time has great admiration for). Despite many funny parodies ('You were a great Cunarder, I/Was only a fishing smack') and ideological high-spirits, the overall impression is of crude propaganda and facile gimmicks, typified in lines such as these:

> Luther and Calvin put in a word
> The god of your priests, they said, is absurd.
> His laws are inscrutable and depend upon grace
> So laissez-faire please for the chosen race.

Three other plays by Auden were all written in collaboration with Christopher Isherwood, and it is not therefore possible to include any detailed study of these in a book devoted solely to Auden. One assumes that he composed the verse in these plays, but one cannot be sure. But since these works did achieve a certain fame and are so closely associated with the left-wing Auden of the Thirties, a brief description of them seems warranted.

'THE DOG BENEATH THE SKIN'

The Dog Beneath the Skin (1935) is a fantasy with both comic and serious treatment, and a certain amount of social satire. The opening chorus sets the village scene:

> The Summer holds: upon its glittering lake
> Lie Europe and the islands; many rivers
> Wrinkling its surface like a ploughman's palm.
> Under the bellies of the grazing horses
> On the far side of posts and bridges
> The vigorous shadows dwindle; nothing wavers.
> Calm at this moment the Dutch sea so shallow
> That sunk St. Pauls would ever show its golden cross
> And still the deep water that divides us still from Norway.
> We would show you at first an English village...

This rather idyllic atmosphere is suitable for the folk-tale Hero, leaving on his Quest for Love, accompanied by his faithful Dog —who is finally revealed as the heir to the village-lands in disguise. The Hero is too much of an idealist and his sentimental vision is corrected by that of his companion who, with his dog's-eye view of society, has experienced the corruption and follies of the village. This fantasy plot enables Auden and Isherwood to introduce a series of satirical figures, such as Miss Iris Crewe of Honeypot Hall, Sir William Spurgeon the Surgeon, H.M. The King of Ostnia, Grabstein a Financier, and Destructive Desmond, whose nightclub act consists of ripping a Rembrandt painting to ribbons with a pocket-knife. Journalism, medical science, religion, monarchy, romantic love, scholarship, pleasure-seekers, and village fascism, are all attacked with a joyous verve in a mishmash of parody, popular songs, choruses, doggerel, slapstick, and melodrama. The parody of a sermon (after which the vicar 'collapses like a wet rag into his chair') was later printed by Auden in his *Collected Poetry* as a serious piece of Christian preaching, to the consternation of many critics. Here is the final paragraph from this sentimental but reactionary vicar:

> 'Oh Father, I am praising Thee, I have always praised Thee, I shall always praise Thee! Listen to the wooden sabots of Thy eager child running to Thy arms! Admit him to the fairs of that blessed country where Thy saints move happily about their neat, clean houses under the blue sky! O windmills, O cocks, O clouds and ponds! Mother is waving from the tiny door! The quilt is turned down in my beautiful blue and gold room! Father, I thank Thee in advance! Everything has been grand! I am coming home!'

'THE ASCENT OF F6'

The Ascent Of F6, described as a 'tragedy in two acts', is mainly in prose. The hero, Michael Ransom, is a mountaineer who is to save England's fair name by climbing F6, a mountain in the Himalayas, at the request of his mother. His feat is a symbolic one and at the top he faces the challenge of the Abbot (and his chanting monks) who asks him to enter the monastery, and there is a climactic scene when Ransom has visionary contact with a mysterious Demon—who is revealed as his mother, when young, singing a lullaby. The suggestion is that England is suffering from an Oedipus complex and that the noble hero,

Ransom, is seeking the consolations of the nursery rather than spiritual truth. Together with this serious allegorical theme, there are scenes of social satire involving peers, generals, society beauties, obsessive radio-listeners, and squabbling mountaineers. Despite the inventive fantasy and stage devices, the play has been strongly criticised for its ambiguity: it is not clear whether Ransom is a hero or not, nor what the play is trying to prove, with its didactic air but confused and confusing technique. The final chorus over the dead body of Ransom fails to clarify the issues:

> Free now from indignation,
> Immune from all frustration
> He lies in death alone;
> Now he with secret terror
> And every minor error
> Has also made Man's weakness known.
>
> Whom history has deserted,
> These have their power exerted,
> In one convulsive throe;
> With sudden drowning suction
> Drew him to his destruction.
> (*Cresc.*) But they to dissolution go.

'ON THE FRONTIER'

On the Frontier (1938) brings together naturalistic scenes in prose, with some telling Shavian debating-matches between articulate businessmen, and brief Expressionist-type choruses in verse. A group of workers, for example, sing a blues with lines such as:

> The lathe on number five has got no safety-guard.
> It's hard to lose your fingers, sister, mighty hard.
>
> Stoke up the fires in furnace number three;
> The day is coming, brother, when we shall all be free!

ACT I PROLOGUE

The frontier is an imaginary line dividing a single room, occupied on one side by the Westland family living under an insane Leader, and on the other by an aristocratic family living under the Ostnia monarchy. As in *Romeo and Juliet* there are a son and a daughter of these two families who fall in love but they cannot meet because of the war between their two homelands. Only after a destructive war can the dying couple meet and unite. The debating-scenes reveal the nature of fascism and its support by businessmen, and the causes of war are satirically displayed. A patriotic song is parodied at one point:

> The mountain has strength, the river has beauty,
>> Westland Science, Religion and Art
> Inspire us with valour and Westland Duty
>> Echoes in every Westland heart!

II, *i*

Amid the political confusion of the proletariat, the cries of two 'left-wing political workers' are heard opposing blind patriotism:

> The country is in danger
> But not from any stranger.
> Your enemies are here
> Whom you should fight, not fear
> For till they cease
> The earth will know no peace.
> Learn to know
> Your friend from foe.

II, *ii*

Nevertheless war comes and it is left to the dying Anna and Eric to present the lesson Auden and Isherwood presumably intend to teach us in this fairly didactic play:

ANNA.   Will people never stop killing each other?
             There is no place in the world
             For those who love.

ERIC.   Believing it was wrong to kill,
             I went to prison, seeing myself
             As the sane and innocent student
             Aloof among practical and violent madmen,
             But I was wrong. We cannot choose our world,
             Our time, our class. None are innocent, none...
             Yet we must kill and suffer and know why.

All errors are not equal. The hatred of our enemies
Is the destructive self-love of the dying,
Our hatred is the price of the world's freedom . . .
But in the lucky guarded future
Others like us shall meet, the frontier gone,
And find the real world happy.

III, iii

These plays by Auden and Isherwood were valiant attempts to create a popular political theatre at a time of European crisis, using devices borrowed from German cabaret sketches, Expressionist drama, and surrealism—verse choruses, dances, music, absurdist humour, Freudian symbolism, and so on. The conventional theatre was plodding along with old-fashioned naturalism, yet the experiments of Auden and Isherwood and others failed to destroy it. (T. S. Eliot in *The Rock*, 1934, *Sweeney Agonistes*, 1932, and *Murder in the Cathedral*, 1935, also tried to introduce new elements into drama, as did Sean O'Casey in *The Silver Tassie*, 1929. Even J. B. Priestley wrote an Expressionist play, *Johnson Over Jordan*, 1939, complete with masked figures.) Perhaps the recent revival of non-naturalistic theatre by writers such as Ionesco, Beckett, Brecht, and their followers, will help to stimulate renewed interest in the plays of Auden and Isherwood.

*   *   *   *   *

Returning now to longer works of which Auden was the sole author, or whose contribution we can be sure of, we may briefly quote two typical stanzas from different sections of the *Letter to Lord Byron* (which is one of the highlights of the volume *Letters from Iceland*, 1937):

Byron, thou should'st be living at this hour!
　　What would you do, I wonder, if you were?
Britannia's lost prestige and cash and power,
　　Her middle classes show some wear and tear,
　　　We've learned to bomb each other from the air;
I can't imagine what the Duke of Wellington
Would say about the music of Duke Ellington . . .

I'm also glad to find I've your authority
　　For finding Wordsworth a most bleak old bore,
Though I'm afraid we're in a sad minority
　　For every year his followers get more,
　　　Their numbers must have doubled since the war.
They come in train-loads to the Lakes, and swarms
Of pupil-teachers study him in *Storm's*.

The whole poem is an exhilarating, sceptical, gossipy discourse on the literary and political scene, together with an autobiographical sketch in which he gently debunks himself, and a successful illustration of his belief that poetry can be good light entertainment. His journey to Iceland was made with Louis MacNeice, and in the Byron pastiche one senses something of MacNeice's talent for fluent, amusing verse-journalism.

'SONNETS FROM CHINA'

For several months in 1938 Auden was with Isherwood in China, which had been attacked by Japan, and they published *Journey to a War* in 1939, which contained in particular a sonnet-sequence and a verse commentary by Auden entitled 'In Time of War'. In the *Collected Shorter Poems* (1966) the commentary is completely dropped, the sequence is re-titled 'Sonnets from China', and many deletions, additions and revisions have been made. In fact, Auden's manipulation of this work is one of the most exasperating he has yet perpetrated. Some of the sonnets were published separately, under helpful titles such as 'Chinese Soldier', 'The Economic Man', or 'Air-raid', but these have given way to uninformative Roman numerals. To show the extent of Auden's rewriting, here are two versions of the opening lines of one sonnet:

The life of man is never quite completed;
The daring and the chatter will go on:
But, as an artist feels his power gone,
These walk the earth and know themselves defeated.

. . . .
Our global story is not yet completed,
Crime, daring, commerce, chatter will go on,
But, as narrators find their memory gone,
Homeless, disterred, these know themselves defeated.

The original title, which now is deleted, was 'Exiles'.

An additional difficulty is Auden's imitation of Rilke's enigmatic style, the unidentified *he*'s, *they*'s and *we*'s, the abrupt beginnings, and the high degree of abstraction aimed at throughout. Sometimes he is apparently talking about a specific person or incident he has witnessed in China, but more often he is ambitiously trying to compress world history into half-a-dozen lines of oblique philosophical commentary. I imagine Auden wanted to capture the abstract form and philosophic density of some Chinese poetry, but despite an impressive tone and images of hypnotic power we remain puzzled about the precise meaning of many of the poems. It is a pity that these remarkable sonnets remain blurred and out of focus. What, for example, can one make of lines like these?

> He stayed, and was imprisoned in possession:
> By turns the seasons guarded his one way,
> The mountains chose the mother of his children,
> In lieu of conscience the sun ruled his day.

It cannot be said that the core of meaning here is easy to come at. Yet there are other sonnets which show what can be achieved in this 'Chinese' style:

> Certainly praise: let song mount again and again
> For life as it blossoms out in a jar or a face,
> For vegetal patience, for animal courage and grace:
> Some have been happy; some, even, were great men.
>
> But hear the morning's injured weeping and know why:
> Ramparts and souls have fallen; the will of the unjust
> Has never lacked an engine; still all princes must
> Employ the fairly-noble unifying lie.
>
> History opposes its grief to our buoyant song,
> To our hope its warning. One star has warmed to birth
> One puzzled species that has yet to prove its worth:
>
> The quick new West is false, and prodigious but wrong
> The flower-like Hundred Families who for so long
> In the Eighteen Provinces have modified the earth.

I am not sure whether the literary form, Poem With Notes, is a modern invention, but Auden has gone one step further in *New Year Letter* by devising Notes With Poem, since the poem occupies fifty-nine pages while the notes run to eighty-two pages (and themselves include poems by Auden). Someone said ironically of Eliot's *The Waste Land* that it was a poetical commentary on the Notes, and Auden presumably intends Poem and Notes to be taken together. (I must in passing say that I have reservations about a poem whose lines only reveal their meaning in an erudite note some scores of pages further on, and one is grateful to Chaucer, Shakespeare and Wordsworth for managing to write intelligibly without this clumsy apparatus of information. In any case Auden's notes, like Eliot's, are not always very helpful; e.g., his note on the lines 'Yet Time can moderate his tone/When talking to a man alone' is: 'In his Diary, Maxim Gorki tells how he came one day unobserved upon Tolstoi, who was attentively regarding a lizard sunning itself on a stone. "Are you happy?" Tolstoi asked the lizard. Then, after looking round to make sure no-one was watching, he said confidentially, "I'm not".'.)

New Year Letter, published in 1941 after Auden had settled in America, is in three parts, and has the air of a chatty disquisition on this-and-that, though Edward Callan claims to find in it a close correspondence with 'Kierkegaard's triad of Aesthetic, Ethical, and Religious Spheres' and a structural resemblance to Dante's *Divine Comedy*. Thus Part I deals with the artist's vocation, Part II with intellectual systems, and Part III with Love restored through Penitence. On the surface, however, this letter reads like the exhilarating conversation of a witty, well-read, enquiring mind, concerned with the problems of humanity, self-critical, alert, and sympathetic. Lightning allusions (in several languages) to Plato, Catullus, Rilke, communism, the Italian invasion of Abyssinia, *Faust*, the quantum theory, etc., etc., are sometimes illuminating, sometimes obscure, for the great difficulty with the poetry of ideas is that the reader may not be as familiar with them as the writer is. (Samuel Butler's *Hudibras*, which has some resemblance to Auden's poem, has long stretches of theological argument which can be appreciated only by rare, erudite readers.) Auden's Notes are a recognition that by itself the poem must remain puzzling to the common reader.

But the poem is also a personal meditation. Part I sees Auden once more questioning the validity of art and the role of the artist when faced with the immense tasks of society:

> Art is not life, and cannot be
> A midwife to society,
> For art is a fait accompli ...

78–80

Art presents us with a 'model' of life, but we must each decide 'To what and how it be applied'. Auden recalls poets of the past, Blake, Dryden, Tennyson, 'whose talents were/For an articulate despair', Baudelaire, Hardy, Rilke, 'whom die Dinge bless/The Santa Claus of loneliness', and, faced with their achievements, recognises his own failings:

> Time and again have slubbered through
> With slip and slapdash what I do,
> Adopted what I would disown,
> The preacher's loose immodest tone ...

219–22

Remembering the anguish of the 'Asiatic cry of pain' and the 'shots of executing Spain' he realises, 'No words men write can stop the war', and yet there is the insistent demand that in some way art should help resolve man's problems. Part II is a complex consideration of intellectual systems, ideologies and Utopias, but the scrutiny of his own successive allegiances to Marx, Freud and now Christianity, finds oblique expression in the sardonic criticism of Wordsworth's similar ideological evolution:

> Thus *Wordsworth* fell into temptation
> In France during a long vacation,
> Saw in the fall of the Bastille
> The Parousia of liberty
> And, weaving a platonic dream
> Round a provincial régime

That sloganised the Rights of Man,
A liberal fellow traveller ran
With sans-culotte and Jacobin
Nor guessed what circles he was in,
But ended, as the devil knew
An earnest Englishman would do,
Left by Napoleon in the lurch,
Supporting the Established Church,
The Congress of Vienna, and
The Squire's paternalistic hand.

649–64

Part III, with the final invocation to the Holy Trinity, and the invitation to 'true love' to join 'the dance', is a complex affirmation of man's spiritual quest to become 'coherent stuff,/Whose form is truth, whose content love . . .'. Out of the excessively elaborate meditation on man's history—the thread of argument is hard to follow—one picks a few key lines: 'Aloneness is man's real condition' or 'true democracy begins/With free confession of our sins', but the overall impression is of uncertainty, despite the invocation to the Trinity and the personal invocation to his 'Dear friend Elizabeth'. It seems that, if the world's problems are to be solved, then one must begin with the guilty soul of the isolated individual:

Instruct us in the civil art
Of making from the muddled heart
A desert and a city where
The thoughts that have to labour there
May find locality and peace,
And pent-up feelings their release.

1676–81

'THE AGE OF ANXIETY'

The theme of the isolated individual receives extended treatment in the 'baroque eclogue' *The Age Of Anxiety* (1948), an ambitious work of more than a hundred pages written in the alliterative stressed verse of Langland's *Piers Plowman* (which is a

144

long account of the search for Christ). Auden's poem is a spiritual quest by four characters through the Seven Ages of Man and the Seven Stages of Human History, but whereas Langland started with a dream in a '*faire felde ful of folke*', Auden locates his characters in a bar on All Souls' Night. The four people, drawn together by loneliness, are: Quant, a widower and a clerk in a shipping office; Malin, a man fatigued by his 'exhausting and idle' job as Medical Intelligence Officer in the Canadian Air Force; Rosetta, a middle-aged lower-middle-class Jewess, who is a buyer in a department store; and Emble, a sexually attractive young man in the Navy. The plot is rudimentary: after several soliloquies the characters converse, undergo a mutual dream, return to Rosetta's flat to celebrate the beginning of an affair between her and Emble; the older men leave, Emble falls asleep, Rosetta realises the affair cannot succeed; the poem closes with the reflections of the men who have departed. It can hardly be called a play and the characters never assume any clear identity. Auden, of course, intended it as a pastoral dream-poem in a highly artificial style, but one cannot help wishing for the structural clarity and flesh-and-blood characterisation of a genuine play to reduce the bewildering effect of incoherence which the work produces. We tend to get lost in a series of meditations, descriptions, songs, parodies, religious rituals, surrealistic fantasies, and verbal extravaganzas.

The virtuosity of scores of passages is undeniable—for example, the thoughts of the Air Force officer on a bombing raid:

> Untalkative and tense, we took off
> Anxious into air; instruments glowed,
> Dials in darkness, for dawn was not yet;
> Pulses pounded; we approached our target . . .
> Bullets were about, blazing anger
> Lunged from below, but we laid our eggs
> Neatly in their nest, a nice deposit
> Which instantly hatched; houses flamed in
> Shuddering sheets as we shed our big
> Tears on their town . . .

p. 18

Auden's talent for parody cleverly uses the alliterative verse to burlesque the clichés of radio commercials:

> Definitely different. Has that democratic
> Extra elegance. Easy to clean.
> Will gladden grand-dad and your girl friend.
> Lasts a lifetime. Leaves no odour.
> American made. A modern product
> Of nerve and know-how with a new thrill.   p. 26

Auden's skill in invoking a scene with a few rapid strokes is much in evidence:

> Peasant wives are pounding
> Linen on stones by a stream,
> And a doctor's silk hat dances
> On top of a hedge as he hurries
> Along a sunken lane.   p. 65

We are frequently reminded of the surrealist passages in Auden's plays when he describes the dream, and there is a similar bizarre treatment of the mock religious ceremony as 'Quant poured out the dregs of the glass on the carpet as a libation and invoked the local spirits'. The comic tone of this section has upset some readers:

> Ye little larvae, lords of the household,
> Potty, P—P, Peppermill, Lampshade,
> Funneybone, Faucet, Face-in-the-wall,
> Head-over-heels and Upsy-daisy
> And Collywobbles and Cupboard-Love,
> Be good, little gods, and guard these lives,   .
>   . . . no filter-passing
> Virus invade; no invisible germ,
> Transgressing rash or gadding tumour
> Attack their tissues . . .   p. 107

One wonders whether this drunken parody of a ritual represents modern superstitions, man's thirst for religious beliefs, or what . . . Similarly, in Malin's final meditation the mixture of the serious and the facetious in his statement of his beliefs is startling and provocative:

For the others, like me, there is only the flash
Of negative knowledge, the night when, drunk, one
Staggers to the bathroom and stares in the glass
To meet one's madness, when what mother said seems
Such darling rubbish and the decent advice
Of the liberal weeklies as lost an art
As peasant pottery ...
... Yet the grossest of our dreams is
No worse than our worship which for the most part
Is so much galimatias to get out of
Knowing our neighbour, all the needs and conceits of
The poor muddled maddened mundane animal
Who is hostess to us all, for each contributes his
Personal panic, his predatory note
To her gregarious grunt as she gropes in the dark
For her lost lollypop.   p. 124

This expression of religious anguish in a verse of rambling syntax and dizzy verbal comedy is typical of Auden's later manner. Perhaps he has invented a new type of 'absurdist' tension between content and style, reflecting the contemporary contradiction between the complex triviality of life and the underlying spiritual hunger of man. This poetry, like that of John Donne, in the 17th century, is calculated to shock and disturb us. On the other hand some critics suspect that Auden's experiment merely exasperates. A French poet once said that in the winter the trees look as though they are made of wood: one might say that Auden's verse looks as though it were made of words, but where have the trees gone? Perhaps into the clotted Milk Wood of Dylan Thomas or into the enchanted forest of verbal entanglement discovered by Christopher Fry (about whom one reviewer nicely commented, 'Fry havoc! and let loose the fogs of words').

One must applaud Auden's strenuous attempts to revive the long poem, and each of his experiments contains exhilarating and original verse. Few, if any, living poets can rival Auden in this endeavour to become, in his own words, a 'minor atlantic Goethe'. To parody the famous lines in *Faust*, may the Eternal Goethean continue to draw him upwards and on.

6

Portraits, Lyrics and Recent Poems

In the days of simpler publishing gimmicks a title such as *The Best of Tennyson* sufficed, but more recently we are offered selections like *The Portmanteau Poe*, or *The Essential Eliot*, with the implication that the modern reader will only have time to imbibe a minimal but effective dose of a writer as he is driven or flown to work. If I had to bow to this trend I would probably call my selection *The Residual Auden*, to indicate that among his profuse output are certain poems which remain as substantial achievements. These poems are of different kinds and belong to different periods of his career, but taken together they give us some idea of his stature as a poet, and enable us to measure the value of his latest work. As we look at these significant landmarks of his art we may conveniently cite the more important of Auden's critics and thus form a picture of Auden's reputation today.

PORTRAITS

In addition to the outstanding successes I have praised during the course of this study (and there were many in each period or genre studied) there are three main groups I would refer to now. The first group consists of poems celebrating specific people, and includes titles such as 'Rimbaud', 'A. E. Housman', 'Edward Lear', 'In Memory of W. B. Yeats', 'In Memory of Ernst Toller', 'Voltaire at Ferney', 'Hermann Melville', 'In Memory of Sigmund Freud', 'Luther', 'Montaigne', and 'At the Grave of Henry James'. These are all retained in the *Collected Shorter Poems* (1966), but earlier volumes offered also 'To E. M. Forster', 'Matthew Arnold', and 'Pascal' (the poem to Forster, somewhat altered, eventually became the final item of *Sonnets from China*).

There are also poems addressed to Benjamin Britten, Chester Kallman, Christopher Isherwood, Erika Mann, Reinhold Niebuhr, Stephen Spender, and 'To T. S. Eliot on his 60th Birthday'.

Auden seems drawn to consider the significance of certain celebrated figures, with some of whom he feels in special sympathy, and his poems usually attempt a succinct presentation of the subject's life and achievement. Matthew Arnold's role is summarised as 'the clear denunciation/Of a gregarious optimistic generation', whereas A. E. Housman is portrayed as one who suppressed personal emotions in the service of Latin scholarship: 'Deliberately he chose the dry-as-dust,/Kept tears like dirty postcards in a drawer.' On the whole the shorter pieces are 'potted biographies' in which the essence of a man is illuminated with epigrammatic economy. Edward Lear was 'a dirty landscape-painter who hated his nose'. Rimbaud gave us 'truth acceptable to lying men'. Henry James is praised as the 'Master of nuance and scruple'.

Among the longer portraits are those of Freud, Voltaire and Yeats, all widely praised by critics. 'In Memory of Sigmund Freud', published in *Kenyon Review* in 1940, is of special interest because of Auden's known use of Freudian ideas. Auden admits that Freud was often 'wrong and, at times, absurd' but it is more obvious now that this 'important Jew who died in exile' is no longer a mere person but 'a whole climate of opinion'. A central passage describes Freudian therapy as basically simple—the recalling of the past and the recognition of tiny events which have led to present unhappiness:

> He wasn't clever at all: he merely told
> the unhappy Present to recite the Past
>   like a poetry lesson till sooner
>   or later it faltered at the line where
>
> long ago the accusations had begun,
> and suddenly knew by whom it had been judged,
>   how rich life had been and how silly,
>   and was life-forgiven and more humble . . .

33–40

And so we all live, thanks to Freud, 'in a world he changed/ simply by looking back with no false regrets . . .'. Auden still sees Freud as a revolutionary force, whose 'technique of unsettlement' has attacked the 'ancient cultures of conceit' and caused the collapse of 'their lucrative patterns of frustration'. Freud is therefore seen as the enemy of the 'Generalised Life', the 'monolith of State' and the 'co-operation of avengers': in other words, Auden believes that the influence of Freud on man and society counteracts some of the huge defects in our civilisation. This leads him to describe evil, which is not

> deeds that must be punished, but our lack of faith,
>   our dishonest mood of denial,
>   the concupiscence of the aggressor.

58–60

It is rather curious that Freudism, usually regarded as atheistic, should encourage a diagnosis of evil in such religious or moral terms—'lack of faith', 'dishonest', and 'concupiscence'. One would think Auden were speaking of Saint Sigmund rather than Dr. Freud.

Optimistically, Auden claims that Freud's pervading influence will help us all. Tired people 'have felt the change in their bones and are cheered', the anxious child 'feels calmer now and somehow assured of escape', and in particular Freud 'would have us remember most of all/to be enthusiastic over the night', not only for the sense of wonder which it offers but also 'because it needs our love'.

Technically the poem is uneven: the winding thread of argument is often stretched to near-breaking point or gets lost among the over-abstract language (e.g. 'our life from whose unruliness/ So many plausible young futures/with threats or flattery ask obedience . . .'). On the other hand the deliberately simple tone (e.g. 'the tyrant tries to/make do with him but doesn't care for him much') varies in effect from memorable statement to chatty emptiness. Nevertheless Auden is dealing with an important theme and is attempting the difficult feat of celebrating, and commenting upon, a whole thought system, without becoming pedantically erudite in a poem which is, after all, an elegy.

'Voltaire at Ferney' (published in *The Listener* in 1939) is a lucid, rapid sketch of a wily but indomitable intellectual hero, waging 'the fight/Against the false and the unfair' and depending in the last resort only on his own determination. Voltaire, like Freud, is another example of a single man persisting, through a life of toil, in the struggle against human evil. Auden sees Voltaire's 'holy war' as a crusade of 'children' against the 'infamous grown-ups', and this image is expanded in the final stanza in which social institutions (and presumably the Catholic Church) are portrayed as sadistic nurses:

> So, like a sentinel, he could not sleep. The night was full of wrong,
> Earthquakes and executions. Soon he would be dead,
> And still all over Europe stood the horrible nurses
> Itching to boil their children. Only his verses
> Perhaps could stop them: He must go on working. Overhead
> The uncomplaining stars composed their lucid song.

25–30

In another poem of the same period, 'In Memory of W. B. Yeats' (who died in January 1939), Auden deliberately flouts the conventions of the traditional elegy. Instead of reassuring us of the poet's worth, the sadness of his friends, and the sympathetic lamenting of Nature, Auden brutally robs us of these normal elegiac comforts by insisting that only a few were aware of his death, that his poems won't change the world, and that Nature remained unconcerned. Auden achieves his effects largely through the cool, objective tone. The wintry scene of deserted airports and snow-disfigured statues is not used as an allegorical picture of Nature mourning. The accident of weather is merely registered by thermometers and laconically reported by the poet:

> What instruments we have agree
> The day of his death was a dark cold day.

5–6

Similarly Yeats's death is matter-of-factly noted as though it were an electric power failure ('The current of his feeling failed') and his personality disintegrates into mere readers' attitudes ('he became his admirers'). Even his poems are subject to human manipulation in the future: 'The words of a dead man/Are modified in the guts of the living.' Not only is Yeats 'silly like us', but the country which inspired him ('Mad Ireland hurt you into poetry') is still as mad, and unchanged by Yeats's verse. Auden here leads us to the harsh truth that the world cannot be put right by poets or their words, 'For Poetry makes nothing happen'.

Only after this honest, if pessimistic, dismissal of the survival chances of the poet and his poetry does Auden affirm, in stanzas which remind us of both Blake and Yeats, that poetry in general remains as a constantly renewed means of persuading man to celebrate his freedom to accept his own limitations. The paradoxical phrases represent the central paradoxes of human life:

> With the farming of a verse
> Make a vineyard of the curse,
> Sing of human unsuccess
> In a rapture of distress;
>
> In the deserts of the heart
> Let the healing fountain start,
> In the prison of his days
> Teach the free man how to praise.

58–65

Poetry seems for Auden to be a force of spiritual regeneration, and the process must begin within man with a change of heart. So this poem, and others in praise of secular saints, indicate Auden's search for religious faith, and poetry itself is seen as playing a spiritual role. It is still to lonely intellects that he ascribes the ability to achieve revolutionary improvements. The Marxist belief in mass movements, perhaps never very strong in Auden, is replaced by an admiration for Yeats, Freud, Voltaire, or Montaigne—of whom he says:

> ...it took
> This donnish undersexed conservative
> To start a revolution and to give
> The Flesh its weapons to defeat the Book.

The second group of poems in my imaginary volume of *Residual Auden* would comprise the universally-praised short lyrics. We have already noted Auden's 'pop' songs, in various traditional and jazz idioms, but there are others which seem nearer to the more conventional literary lyric—though in Auden's hands they are hardly 'conventional'. Critics find it rather hard to say much about lyrics, as their simplicity of form and direct musical appeal defy analysis. Monroe K. Spears can describe 'May with its light behaving' with technical precision: '... seven-line stanzas using consonance instead of rime, in the pattern abcddbc, with trimeter as a metrical basis, lengthening occasionally to tetrameter and employing frequent feminine endings'—but we have to turn to the poem itself to experience these devices as living words. This particular poem, now entitled 'May', and first published in *The Listener* in 1935, has a deceptively simple song quality, but is really quite a complex piece of writing. The opening lines are ambiguous, for the 'light behaving' of May could mean the behaviour of daylight or morally light behaviour, and the 'vessel' which is stirred is thus probably the sexual organ. The picnics near the 'swan-delighting river' attract the 'singular and sad' who are 'willing to recover', which suggests that Auden is again referring to neurotics who, for once, are willing their own cure. In contrast to the renewed life of Maytime the dead past is 'remote and hooded', a region of 'vague words' and forests where children meet and white angel-vampires flit. Presumably these symbols are meant to imply that for the modern generation the traditions of the older society, and the childhood world of supernatural belief, are both dead. There has been another Fall and man has eaten the apple from the forbidden tree: 'we ... /Stand now with shaded eye,/The dangerous apple taken.' Auden is having to rely on symbolic images, such as 'vague words' or 'white angel-vampires', to make his meaning clear and one questions whether he is being explicit enough.

The real world which confronts fallen, but mature, man is no paradise but a place haunted by the Death Wish, peopled by the unjust, and a stage where a 'dying Master sinks tormented/In his admirers' ring'—again the reference is not entirely clear. The final stanza returns to the theme of love, an instinct, we are reminded, which man shares with the 'impatient/Tortoise and roe'. But love, which had seemed to offer hope to lonely neurotics, is pronounced inadequate. In the face of moral problems (if that is what the vague line 'Before the evil and the good' means) human love is of no avail:

> How insufficient is
> Touch, endearment, look.

So what promised to be a jolly traditional lyric about love in springtime is revealed as a slightly enigmatic, pessimistic comment on Fallen Man—a remarkable achievement, despite the obscurities. (Incidentally, the 1966 version, which I have quoted, is a modified one. For example: the earlier 'Animal motions of the young,/The common wish for death' becomes the less precise 'Brave motions of the young,/Abundant wish for death.')

Another lyric, also published first in *The Listener* in 1935, is 'Look, stranger, on this island now', which was given the title 'Seascape' when it was set to music by Benjamin Britten. Actually the poem does not need a setting because it has a complex, haunting music of its own. Perhaps the most amazing thing about this poem is the way the imagery, even the consonants and vowels, are carefully chosen for their sound-effects. There is a fusion of visual and aural in such phrases as: 'May wander like a river/The swaying sound of the sea.' One has only to read aloud such clusters of visual, aural and tactile effects as 'chalk wall falls', or 'the pluck/And knock of the tide', to be reminded of the pure word-music experiments of Edith Sitwell (whose *Façade* pieces, spoken through a megaphone to Walton's music, had caused Noël Coward to walk out in disgust). But Auden's poem is no mere exercise in consonant-juggling. What he evokes is a mood of reverie or contemplation, in which the speaker, characteristically remote from the distant ships 'like floating seeds', becomes immersed in the rhythms of nature, in the hypnotic movement of the shingle, scrambling after the sucking surf, or the giddy experience of the gull which 'lodges/A moment' on the sheer side of the chalk cliff. Completely undidactic, the poem simply invites us to enter the world of the non-human with all our senses awake. It is all done by technical devices, but the result is one of inexplicable wonder.

'Fish in the unruffled lakes' was published in *The Listener* in 1936 and also set to music by Britten. Like many of Auden's poems it has the theme of the contrast between human beings and animals, and it divides neatly into three stanzas, each with its own minor theme. The animal creation is pictured in the first stanza as being beautiful and perfect. The fish wear 'swarming colours', the swans have a 'white perfection', and the lion walks through his 'innocent grove': they simply live and then disappear on 'Time's toppling wave'. Auden's vision of animal existence does not pause to consider 'Nature red in tooth and claw' (as Tennyson put it) nor the diseases and natural calamities to which animals are subject, and so we may not quite agree with him when, in stanza two, he presents the human condition as one of self-conscious anguish, produced by man's moral sense ('Duty's conscious wrong') or his awareness of time ('The Devil in the clock'). His conclusion is that imperfect and unhappy man must lose his loves and 'On each beast and bird that moves/Turn an envious look'. But whereas in 'May' the poet had asserted that love was inadequate, here the final stanza celebrates a woman whose capacity to bestow love freely raises her above the 'animal' perfection she already has:

> But I must bless, I must praise
> That you, my swan, who have
> All gifts that to the swan
> Impulsive Nature gave,
> Last night should add
> Your voluntary love.

With something of the emotion-charged logic of a Metaphysical poem, Auden has successfully combined philosophic argument with lyrical poignancy to produce a memorable, original piece on the oldest of topics.

Finally we may consider the well-known 'Lay your sleeping

head, my love' (later called 'Lullaby'), published in *New Writing* in 1937. The poem opens with a slow, reflective stanza which accepts the beauty of love in a mood of clear-eyed realisation of its imperfections:

> Lay your sleeping head, my love,
> Human on my faithless arm . . .
> But in my arms till break of day
> Let the living creature lie,
> Mortal, guilty, but to me
> The entirely beautiful.

Although love itself is a common enough experience—lovers lie in 'their ordinary swoon'—it does, claims Auden, offer man extraordinary visions of 'supernatural sympathy,/Universal love and hope', and in particular it affords the hermit both an 'abstract insight' and a 'sensual ecstasy'. These are large claims to make in a love lyric, and one is a little disappointed at the generalised expressions which mar the otherwise novel style. The third stanza is vigorously declamatory, not to say melodramatic and obscure in its references—who exactly are the 'fashionable madmen' who raise their 'pedantic boring cry'? At all events the impression remains that love is somehow a refuge from the stupidities and dangers of life. The final stanza, indeed, indicates that the experience of love is essentially fleeting, for 'Beauty, midnight, vision dies', and as the lovers wake and return to the daylight world, the poet asks that they should accept the real, but imperfect existence that human beings must lead:

> Let the winds of dawn that blow
> Softly round your dreaming head
> Such a day of welcome show
> Eye and knocking heart may bless,
> Find our mortal world enough . . .

The brief selection from Auden's love lyrics therefore suggests that even while submitting to the haunting, melodic idiom of this traditional genre, he is able to consider with philosophic seriousness the meaning of human affection and to offer us his vision and wisdom. Those who enjoy the love poems of

Shakespeare, Donne, Marvell or Rilke, where the celebration of Eros goes hand in hand with a reflective meditation upon the significance of love, will surely find Auden's work congenial.

AUDEN'S LATE STYLE

The final group of poems I would like to study mainly represents Auden's current achievement in a special style, which has appeared in poems here and there throughout most of his career, but which has now become characteristic of his latest writings. This 'late Auden style' features a relaxed tone, a curious mixture of pedantic terms and slang, and long, complicated sentences which wind their way lazily through a variety of stanza forms. One imagines that Auden has been influenced by the informal meditational manner found in Eliot's *Four Quartets*, and by the celebrated sinuous style of Henry James, whose novels he admires. Not everybody likes Auden's latest stylistic experiment, and hostile critics have objected to his pilfering of dictionaries for abstruse terms, to his frivolous chattiness, and to his syntactical doodling. Obviously there are dangers in Auden's deliberate attempt to be offhand and one must certainly ask how far the casual surface-effects only reflect a basically facetious attitude to experience, or a disarmingly chummy refusal to take life seriously. Is Auden merely a sophisticated entertainer, adroitly exploiting a modish taste for offbeat poetic dilettantism, or does he, as John Holloway claims, significantly register 'the civilisation of our century more comprehensively than any other poet who has written in English'? Space permits only a brief selection from Auden's recent volumes, but this will be sufficient to enable us to gauge the quality of his mature work.

Taking them in the order of their publication, we may begin with 'In Praise of Limestone', which first appeared in *Horizon*, July 1948, and subsequently in the volume *Nones* (1952), which is the text I shall use. G. S. Fraser (in his essay, 'The Career of W. H. Auden') has called it 'one of the most beautiful of all his recent poems', and Barbara Everett similarly extols it. As she says in her *Auden*, the triumph of this new style 'lies in the leisurely, apparently casual but in fact deliberate, winding movement towards a quiet climax that is half denied by, but half resists, the profusion of circumstantial detail that precedes it'. Because of the very nature of the style and the leisurely devices it is almost impossible to do justice to this poem without quoting it in full. In an almost languid, conversational manner Auden describes the geology of an area for which 'we the inconstant ones' are homesick:

> Mark these rounded slopes
>   With their surface fragrance of thyme and beneath
> A secret system of caves and conduits; hear these springs
>   That spurt out everywhere with a chuckle
> Each filling a private pool for its fish and carving
>   Its own little ravine whose cliffs entertain
> The butterfly and the lizard ...

3–9

Into these sober passages Auden injects however some disconcerting thoughts. This landscape, described above, is unexpectedly compared to human beings:

> What could be more like Mother or a fitter background
>   For her son, for the nude young male who lounges
> Against a rock displaying his dildo, never doubting
>   That for all his faults he is loved ...

11–14

Auden is really using Nature as a metaphor for Man. The convolutions of the landscape represent the people who 'become a pimp/Or deal in fake jewellery or ruin a fine tenor voice', the granite suggests the hard ascetic life from which 'Saints-to-be/ Slipped away sighing', and the clays and gravels offer themselves as plains on which armies can drill. In this oblique, original and amusing way, Auden tells us about the nature of man by apparently giving us a geology lesson. Finally, on a personal and religious note, the poem reaches a quiet, but moving climax by speaking of love and a future existence in terms of such seemingly prosaic things as water and rock:

> Dear, I know nothing of
> Either, but when I try to imagine a faultless love

Or the life to come, what I hear is the murmur
Of underground streams, what I see is a limestone landscape.

90–3

'The Managers', published in *Horizon*, November 1948, and later in *Nones*, mingles the snapshot imagery of the earlier, social verse with the winding sentence-structure of the emerging style. It is a poem of immediate appeal, in which Auden contrasts the glamorous, bigger-than-life 'genuine Caesars' of the past, with the modern wielders of power—'quiet/Men, working too hard in rooms that are too big.' Not for them the pleasure of 'huge meals' or palaces full of girls:

> A neat little luncheon
> Of sandwiches is brought to each on a tray,
>   Nourishment they are able
> To take with one hand without looking up
>   From papers a couple
> Of secretaries are needed to file,
>   From problems no smiling
> Can dismiss . . .

32–9

Auden describes our bureaucratic leaders with sad distaste, in disillusionment rather than anger, and offers them no pity. After all, this élite group will have, unlike the rest of us, 'places on the last/Plane out of disaster'.

This poem retains something of the social criticism of Auden of the Thirties. 'Lakes', first published in *New Poems by American Poets*, 1953, and reprinted in *The Shield of Achilles*, 1955, forms part of a series called 'Bucolics', seven poems in different metres and displaying once more Auden fecund originality. These 'Bucolics' are not conventional pastoral verses but philosophic meditations on natural forces and the qualities in man that they symbolise (a method we have already seen in the earlier 'In Praise of Limestone'). Of the seven, 'Lakes' is perhaps the least serious. This is in keeping with the theme that lakes are human and cosy in contrast to the 'estranging sea'. This 'cosiness' is reflected in the deliberately homely notion that Nature is to be measured by Man, as the opening lines comically declare:

> A lake allows an average father, walking slowly,
>> To circumvent it in an afternoon,
> And any healthy mother to halloo the children
>> Back to her bedtime from their games across ...

1–4

This informal manner allows Auden to range freely over many topics—the fortune-scarred history of Christendom, Poseidon, a play by Webster, water-scorpions, Jack and Jill—which gives his poetry the appeal of lively, intelligent conversation. The danger here is of whimsicality. Can we seriously accept his assertion that the moral influence of lakes is so powerful that 'Foreign Ministers should always meet beside one', as it will provoke a 'physical compassion' that will help to unite their respective armies? Wordsworth really believed that Nature had a beneficial effect on Man: Auden himself seems to suggest that he has merely been indulging in a sentimental fantasy as he, with jocular pedantry, lists the curious names for lakes and admits, in the final self-mocking line, that it is something of a game:

> It is unlikely I shall ever keep a swan
>> Or build a tower on any small tombolo,
> But that's not going to stop me wondering what sort
>> Of lake I would decide on if I should.
> Moraine, pot, oxbow, glint, sink, crater, piedmont, dimple ...?
>> Just reeling off their names is ever so comfy.

49–54

There are many examples of Auden's latest style in the collection *About the House*, published in 1966. We have already looked at the humorous, personal poem 'On the Circuit', and briefly referred to 'Grub first, then Ethics (Brecht)' (which originally was called 'On Installing an American Kitchen in Lower Austria'). Many of these poems are dedicated to personal friends, and there is one set of verses which is devoted to each room in Auden's house. The poem on the meditative influence of the privy is appropriately written for Auden's old friend Christopher Isherwood, who for many years has practised Hindu meditation in California, whereas 'The Cave of Making' is a moving, chatty, but unsentimental elegy upon his friend and collaborator Louis MacNeice. It is in this poem that Auden refers to his own poetic ambitions:

> . . . I should like to become, if possible,
> a minor atlantic Goethe,
> with his passion for weather and stones but without his silliness
> re the Cross: at times a bore, but
> while knowing Speech can at best, a shadow echoing
> the silent light, bear witness
> to the Truth it is not, he wished it were, as the Francophile
> gaggle of pure songsters
> are too vain to.

91–9

This passage, incidentally, illustrates the meandering syntax of the later Auden. It has a pleasant, ruminative quality, though, as in the final lines, it can seem almost incoherent.

This 1966 collection stresses the personal and domestic aspects of life and reflects perhaps a belief that public order is built upon private virtue, and that the integrity of individual existence is to be respected and celebrated. No doubt some critics feel that Auden has deserted the social scene, and the public role of moralist and satirist, for the quietist pastime of whimsical armchair-philosophising in the seclusion of his Austrian farmhouse. Although in fact Auden continues to write prolifically, and to make extensive lecture tours, one cannot deny that his current poetry lacks the urgent note of his Thirties verse, and his attack on modern values is usually oblique. In 'Et in Arcadia Ego', for instance, the apparent taming of Nature and Man over the centuries is delicately suggested in this stanza about placid living, controlled by Religion and Time:

> A church clock subdivides the day,
> Up the lane at sundown
> Geese podge home.

16–18

The underplaying in these lines is deliberate. Auden is no longer the strident prophet of 'Spain', but the low-voiced, meditating conversationalist. I am sure that the tactics are consciously adopted and that Auden's calculated reticence is intended to make us silence our blaring T.V. sets and listen to his quiet, but impressive, comments and warnings. It is as though, in a noisy world of competing demagogues and mass media, the poet's only strategy is to whisper. It is a risk, of course, for the Christian to trust that 'Blessed is he that whispers, for he shall be heeded', but it looks as though Auden is prepared to take such a risk.

About the House closes with 'Whitsunday in Kirchstetten', published originally in December 1962 in *The Reporter*. This poem begins with a description of Auden at Catholic Mass in the Austrian village where he spends his summers, mingling homely details with ironical reflections:

> *Komm Schöpfer Geist* I bellow as Herr Beer
> picks up our slim offerings and Pfarrer Lustkandl
>   quietly gets on with the Sacrifice
> as Rome does it: outside car-worshippers enact
>   the ritual exodus from Vienna
> their successful cult demands (though reckoning time
>   by the Jewish week and the Christian year
> like their pedestrian fathers).

1–8

The colloquial humour and the winding sentences are typical of Auden's recent verse, as are the erudite allusions and unusual words (some of which do not appear in Webster's *Dictionary*, 1966 edition). Most readers would have to be told that *Pfarrer* is a parish priest; *metic*, an alien resident of an Ancient Greek city; *Gemütlichkeit*, good-natured disposition; *hazing*, to harass; *menalty*, middle class; *papabile*, Italian for 'qualified and likely to become Pope'; *magnalia*, wonderful works; *Crimtartary*, a rather vague area in Central Asia; *Geist* and *Esprit*, German and French words for spirit; and *trousered Africa* presumably means 'put Africans into trousers'.

Several of these expressions are pronounced *rare and obsolete* by the Oxford English Dictionary and the semi-colloquial term *hazing* can also mean 'to make hazy' or even 'to drive animals from horseback'. Some critics have denounced Auden for this eccentric ransacking of dictionaries, forgetting that many of the greatest poets have had a wicked eye for the hidden charms of language. Also, in an age of journalistic cliché and bureaucratic jargon, surely it is the poet's chivalric duty (and pleasure) to rescue distressed diction and stamp his verses with a personal idiom? Certainly there is the danger of pedantry or preciosity, but Auden seems to me to be resurrecting relevant terms with good taste as well as exhilaration. (One would not like every poet to do this, just as one does not admire the imitators of Eliot and Pound who spatter their pages with Sanskrit and Chinese.)

One of the virtues of Auden's new style, as we see in 'Whitsunday in Kirchstetten', is the easy movement from personal anecdote to graver general reflections, from jocular remarks about old notions of God ('the Big White Christian upstairs') to ironical comments on worship:

> An altar bell makes a noise
> as the Body of the Second Adam
> is shown to some of his torturers . . .

54–6

The importance of Auden's achievement in this poem is that he is able to be amusing, serious, erudite, personal, gossipy, political and religious within the compass of two and a half pages of verse. His deeper concerns are with society ('whether the world has improved /is doubtful, but we believe it could . . .'), with today's political menace ('where minefield and watchtower say NO EXIT/from peace-loving Crimtartary'), and with modern forms of inhumanity ('it could be the looter's turn/for latrine duty and the flogging block . . .'). Auden is aware of the anguish of existence, though in the last resort he responds with a Christian affirmation of faith and joy, delicately understated:

> . . . about
> catastrophe or how to behave in one

I know nothing, except what everyone knows—
if there when Grace dances, I should dance.

77–80

ACHIEVEMENT

With this remarkable religious poem we must leave our study of
the past achievements of this versatile, commanding figure and
turn again to the little magazines where his current poems are
appearing (no doubt to be exasperatingly chopped and changed
before being published in a collected edition). We shall continue to
look forward with more than curiosity to his evolving talent as
it invents new forms and explores new experiences. It would be
hard to forecast the next stage in Auden's poetic journey, but if
'Moralities' (in *London Magazine*, February 1968) is any indication, he is experimenting with didactic pop songs based on
Aesop. Jack McGrew, who has come to woo Jill, the oil-king's
daughter, has

> Come from afar in his motor-car,
>   Eager to show devotion,
> Looking so cute in his Sunday suit,
>   And smelling of shaving-lotion.

Auden is a serious writer who has demonstrated to us that
poetry can be fun. His urgent social verse, his virtuosity in the
field of ballads, songs and lyrics, his introspective manifestos,
and his original, ambitious long poems make him for me, despite
his obscurities and failures, a poet of compelling interest, as
significant for our day as Eliot and Yeats were for an earlier
generation. But one must add that, on the whole, critics have
been puzzled about Auden, and in particular the *Scrutiny* school
has consistently attacked him. In the 1950 edition of *New Bearings
in English Poetry* F. R. Leavis still insisted that Auden 'has hardly
come nearer to essential maturity since, though he made a rapid
advance in sophistication'. It would be easy to compile a publisher's anti-blurb of hostile comments. For example, D. J. Enright,
in *The Apothecary's Shop*, 1957, likened Auden's manner to that
of the Ancient Mariner, for 'the reader is pinned against the wall'

by his heavy moralising. C. B. Cox and A. E. Dyson, in *Modern Poetry*, 1963, say trenchantly that 'he had not the kind of imagination needed to understand the consciousness of the workers whose cause he championed'. John Bayley, in *The Romantic Survival*, 1957, makes the adverse point that 'though Auden never regards people wantonly or inhumanly he does depersonalise them and transform them into a bizarre extension of object or place'. R. G. Cox, in *The Pelican Guide to English Literature 7*, 1961, believes that Auden 'has not been able to resist the irrelevant elaboration, the chasing of too many hares at once, the smart epigram, or the multiplication of self-conscious ironies'. Although John Lehmann praises Auden in his autobiographical *The Whispering Gallery*, 1955, he does also add that 'the transplantation to America dried up the sensuous sap and made his utterances for a time seem more like the delphic riddling of a disembodied mind'. A most pungent critic is A. Alvarez, who, in *The Shaping Spirit*, 1961, writes damningly: 'He has caught one tone of his period, but it is a cocktail party tone, as though most of his work were written off the cuff for the amusement of his friends.'

Each reader will come to his own conclusions about the value of Auden's work. I have offered my own praise and blame only as a contribution to the critical give-and-take, which, one hopes, stimulates us to a more sensitive reading of his poems. It would be particularly interesting to know what people who have been closely associated with Auden think of his later verse, and I am happy to be able to record the reactions of two men whose careers have been intimately connected with Auden's. Geoffrey Grigson, whose *New Verse* featured so much of Auden's early work, kindly communicated with me, on 28 March 1969, from England, in response to a request to evaluate the 'later Auden':

I greatly admire and revere W.H.A., but I don't think I can do what you ask: for one thing I don't divide him—for another thing though I do suspect the pressure to poems has weakened in him over the years, I wouldn't be sure without knowing better than I do all the verse he has published in the late fifties and sixties. It would be natural enough anyway; but then pressure can mount again, and a 'poet' does consist of his best poems whatever happens, whatever he produces, in between the best.

Auden's friend Rex Warner, writing on the same day but from Connecticut, U.S.A., very generously sent his personal and critical appraisal which seems to me an admirable account of an outstanding poet of our day:

Of course I knew him well at Oxford and until he went to America. After that I only met him once, I think, until I came here myself about 6 years ago. Since then I've met him several times, in fact twice quite recently. My main impression is that he has changed (except in appearance) so little from the early days. He has always combined a great kindliness with a strange sort of dogmatism which expresses itself in sets of rules, categories, exhortations and prohibitions. It reminds me of a good headmaster, anxious for the welfare of the boys, and at the same time insistent on sound scholarship and the 'truths' of religion. Perhaps because of his great and unflagging intellectual dexterity and energy, these rules are constantly being reformulated, but always with genial authority. I miss the purely lyric impulse found in, say, 'Look Stranger', and I don't agree with him when he dismisses the political poems on Spain as worthless. But he's very consistent with the set of rules which was for him at the time operative. I think his criticism suffers from this compulsive classificatory method, but in spite of it he is always saying something fresh and inspiring. In fact it may be that this self-adjustable intellectual strait-jacket is actually a help. He always inspires great affection in all who know him.

Bibliography

AUDEN'S WORKS (published by Faber & Faber unless otherwise stated)

1928 *Poems* (handprinted at Oxford by Stephen Spender)

1930 *Poems*

1932 *The Orators*

1933 *Poems* (seven poems in 1930 edition replaced by others)

1933 *The Dance of Death*

1934 *Poems* (includes *Poems, 1933; Paid on Both Sides; The Orators; The Dance of Death*)

1935 *The Dog Beneath the Skin* (with Isherwood)

1936 *The Ascent of F6* (with Isherwood)

1936 *Look, Stranger!* (published as *On This Island*, New York: Random House, 1937)

1937 *Spain*

1937 *Letters from Iceland* (with MacNeice)

1938 *On the Frontier* (with Isherwood)

1938 *Selected Poems*

1939 *Journey to a War* (with Isherwood)

1940 *Another Time*

1940 *Some Poems*

1941 *New Year Letter* (published as *The Double Man*, New York: Random House, 1941)

1945 *For the Time Being*

1945 *The Collected Poetry of W. H. Auden* (New York: Random House, 1945. Faber, 1948)

1948 *The Age of Anxiety*

1950 *Collected Shorter Poems 1930–1944*

1951 *The Enchaféd Flood*

1952 *Nones*
1954 *Mountains*
1955 *The Shield of Achilles*
1956 *The Old Man's Road* (New York: Voyages Press)
1960 *Homage to Clio*
1963 *The Dyer's Hand*
1966 *About the House*
1966 *Collected Shorter Poems 1927–1957*
1968 *Collected Longer Poems*
1968 *Secondary Worlds*

MAJOR CRITICAL STUDIES

Joseph Warren Beach: *The Making of the Auden Canon* (Univ. of Minnesota Press, 1957).

John G. Blair: *The Poetic Art of W. H. Auden* (Princeton Univ. Press, 1965).

Barbara Everett: *Auden* (Oliver & Boyd, 1964).

Richard Hoggart: *Auden: An Introductory Essay* (Chatto & Windus, 1964).

Justin Replogle: *Auden's Poetry* (Methuen, 1969).

Monroe K. Spears (ed.): *Auden: A Collection of Critical Essays* (Prentice-Hall, 1964).

Monroe K. Spears: *The Poetry of W. H. Auden: The Disenchanted Island* (Oxford Univ. Press, 1968).

OTHER CRITICAL STUDIES

A. Alvarez: *The Shaping Spirit* (Chatto & Windus, 1961), Chapter IV, 'W. H. Auden: Poetry and Journalism'.

John Bayley: *The Romantic Survival* (Constable, 1960), Chapter IX. 'W. H. Auden'.

J. M. Cohen: *Poetry of This Age 1908–1958* (Hutchinson, 1960).

C. B. Cox and A. E. Dyson: *Modern Poetry: Studies in Practical Criticism* (Edward Arnold, 1963).

R. G. Cox: 'The Poetry of W. H. Auden', in *The Pelican Guide to English Literature*, 7, 1964.

Dennis Enright: *The Apothecary's Shop* (Secker & Warburg, 1957), 'Reluctant Admiration: A Note on Auden and Rilke'.

John Fuller: 'Private Faces in Private Places', in *London Magazine*,
V, 11, Feb. 1966, pp. 116–20.

John Holloway: 'The Master as Joker', in *Art International*, XIII,
1, Jan. 1969, pp. 17–20.

Randall Jarrell: 'Changes of Attitude and Rhetoric in Auden's
Poetry', in *Southern Review*, VII, Autumn 1941, pp. 326–49.

Randall Jarrell: 'Freud to Paul: The Stages of Auden's Ideology',
in *Partisan Review*, XII, Fall 1945, pp. 437–57.

F. R. Leavis: 'Auden, Bottrall and Others', in *Scrutiny*, III, 1,
June 1934, pp. 70–83.

Louis MacNeice: *Modern Poetry* (Oxford Univ. Press, 1968).

John Mander: *The Writer and Commitment* (Secker & Warburg,
1961), Chapter I, 'Must we burn Auden?'

Allan Rodway: 'Logicless Grammar in Audenland', in *London
Magazine*, IV, 12, March 1965, pp. 31–44.

Alan Ross: *Poetry 1945–1950* (Longmans, Green & Co., 1951).

N. A. Scott: 'The Poetry of Auden', in *London Magazine*, VIII,
1, Jan. 1961, pp. 44–63.

Stephen Spender: *The Creative Element* (Hamish Hamilton, 1953),
Chapter VIII, 'The Theme of Political Orthodoxy in the
'Thirties'.

C. K. Stead: 'Auden's "Spain"', in *London Magazine*, VII, 12,
March 1968 pp. 41–54.

FOR FURTHER READING

W. H. Auden (ed.): *Kierkegaard* (Cassell, 1955). A selection with
an introduction by Auden.

George Barker: *Collected Poems 1930–1955* (Faber & Faber, 1957).

Christopher Caudwell: *Studies in a Dying Culture* (John Lane,
1948).

C. Day-Lewis: *Collected Poems 1929–1933* (Hogarth Press, 1938).

C. Day-Lewis: *The Buried Day* (Chatto & Windus, 1960).
Autobiography.

Reuben Fine: *Freud: A Critical Re-Evaluation of His Theories*
(Allen & Unwin, 1963).

Robert Graves and Alan Hodge: *The Long Week-End. A Social
History of Great Britain 1918–1939* (Faber & Faber, 1940).

Geoffrey Grigson (ed.): *New Verse* (reprint by Kraus Corporation, 1966)

Georg Groddeck: *Exploring the Unconscious* (Vision Press, 1966).

Granville Hicks *et al.* (eds.): *Proletarian Literature in the United States. An Anthology* (Martin Lawrence Ltd., n.d.).

Richard Hoggart: *W. H. Auden: A Selection* (Hutchinson, 1961).

Christopher Isherwood: *Lions and Shadows* (Signet Modern Classics, 1968). Contains a sketch of Auden as 'Hugh Weston', pp. 112–21.

John Lehmann: *Collected Poems 1930–64* (Eyre & Spottiswoode, 1963).

John Lehmann: *The Whispering Gallery. Autobiography I* (Longmans, Green & Co., 1955).

Malcolm Muggeridge: *The Thirties* (Hamish Hamilton, 1940).

Reuben Osborn: *Freud and Marx* (Gollancz, 1937).

Eric Allen Osborne (ed.): *In Letters of Red* (Michael Joseph, 1938).

Robin Skelton (ed.): *Poetry of the Thirties* (Penguin Books, 1964).

Stephen Spender: *Collected Poems 1928–1953* (Faber & Faber, 1955).

Stephen Spender: *World Within World: The Autobiography of Stephen Spender* (Readers Union Ltd., 1953).

Stephen Spender and John Lehmann (eds.): *Poems for Spain* (Hogarth Press, 1939).

David Thomson: *England in the Twentieth Century* (Penguin Books, 1966).

Index